MOUNTAIN SOJOURNS

A Journal of over Forty Hikes and Rides in the Prescott Area

Ronald H. Smith

CASTLE ROCK
PUBLISHING

Liability Disclaimer

In assembling the information for this field guide I have provided specifics of trail conditions, distances, estimates of difficulty, and an occasional warning. Much of this information is based on my subjective judgement and that of others who assisted on this project. Consequently, the information is subject to errors in judgement, typographical errors, equipment variability, and changes on the land itself. Therefore, in using this guide and in traveling the trails described, it is incumbent on each individual to exercise good judgement and caution. The author and others either directly or indirectly associated with this publication will assume no liability for accident, injury, damage, or other losses that might occur to persons reading this book. Traveling in remote, rough country always involves elements of risk to personal health and safety. These risks can be minimized through careful trip planning and cautious travel on the trails.

Typesetting, text design, graphics, and layout: Castle Rock Publishing, 1712 Pine Woods Road, Prescott, Arizona (602) 445-6678. Obtain copies of this book by writing or calling the above address.

Pen & ink illustrations: Dee Cantlon

Cover photograph: Larry Kantor

Table of Contents

Acknowledgements

Although I cruised many of the trails described here alone, companions were crucial to conducting one-way trips on many of the longer trails. Vehicles needed to be shuttled and side trails explored. Personal safety also suggests that one not travel alone in remote country. John Mock assisted me on a number of trails and was a durable, cheerful and intelligent trail-mate. I am greatly indebted for his contribution to this book. Likewise, my wife Loraine was both a traveling companion and taxi service. I could not nor would I have wished to finish this project without her company. Other trail companions included Ron ("Flash") Gordon, Jan Gordon, Doug Perkins, and Mary Curran Perkins.

In compiling much of the background information for this guide I have relied on the advice and expertise of a number of people. I want to thank staff and field personnel of the Prescott National Forest, but especially Bill Townsend, Beverly Morgan, Dave and Cheryl Rudolph, and Doug Vandergon.

My thanks also goes to Annette Clift for maps of local trails, to Angelo and Peggy Ossanna for a shuttle to a trailhead and a critical tip about an unmarked trail which I subsequently hiked and described in this book. My thanks also to a most congenial Mike Wurtz for helping me to get started in the Sharlot Hall Museum Archives.

A special thanks to Jerry Ellsworth who has probably saved me from my own fractured syntax with a thorough editing of my manuscript.

Finally, I want to thank a friend of some 15 years, Paul Borscheidt, for sharing his knowledge of computers and software. Without his advice I would probably be still mired in that black hole of unexplained system crashes and cryptic error messages.

Preface

"If our generation exploits everything available—the trees, the water, or the minerals—without any care for the coming generations and the future, then we are at fault, aren't we? But if we have a genuine sense of universal responsiblility as our central motivation, then our relating with the environment will be well-balanced."

—*The Dalai Lama, Tenzin Gyatso*

THERE ARE MANY LEGITIMATE BENEFITS TO BE DERIVED FROM TRAIL WALKING OR RIDING. Among these are exercise and cardio-vascular conditioning. The outdoor experience can reinforce friendships among traveling companions and reduce stress. There is also offer the pleasure of views, or the feeling of accomplishment of the accumulated miles.

There is another dimension, however, to trail hiking or riding that can transcend all of the above. This aspect has more to do with soul. Being "in the country" offers a real opportunity to become more intimately connected to the ground that bears our footsteps. More than simply a process to follow, it is an attitude with which we enter wild places. It involves a state of mind that expands our consciousness and makes us more sensitive to the things that we see.

With this attitude comes a greater awareness of how we personally impact the areas we travel. With increased awareness we also become better able to see the impacts of other land uses such as livestock grazing, fuelwood and timber extraction, mining, off-road vehicle use, watershed management, residential development, and recreational use. Without that spiritual connection to the earth, it is much more difficult to develop strategies for managing or protecting our landscape resources for our generation or future generations. For this, after all, is our landscape, our habitat. If we plunder it for short term gain, we only endanger the sustained use of these resources and our ultimate existence here.

So, walk or ride these trails with a sense of intimacy rather than domination or accomplishment. Let the wind and rain on your face, the cactus spine in your calf, or mud on your boots be part of your covenant with wild places. Build on this relationship with our habitat by immersing yourself in it, and then rejecting those activities that tend only to violate its integrity.

—*Ron Smith*
January 1993

How to use this book

SOME OF THESE SUGGESTIONS MAY SEEM SELF-EVIDENT, but most teachers say that repetition reinforces behavior. so — rule #1 is: take it with you.

I have used a uniform format for describing each trail. A *General Description* section presents some attributes of a trail and the country it passes through, just to gain for the traveler some criteria for deciding whether this area would be worth exploring.

This guide is organized into geographic sections, all within approximately a 30 mile radius of Prescott. Also, many of the trails offer access to a significant geographic feature such as Granite Mountain or the Bradshaw Mountains.

By grouping trails by area, I was able to more easily relate neighboring or connecting trails and place these on a single composite map. Those maps will follow the descriptions of trails drawn on them.

Access to Trailhead Location describes road and highway access to the more commonly used or most easily approached trailhead location. To provide some uniformity in describing how to reach a particular trail I have used *downtown Prescott* as a point of origin. More specifically this means the corner of Montezuma and Gurley Streets. In general, I have made reference in those descriptions to roadway and trail signs as they existed when this book went to press. Trail signs, however, are particularly transient as the trails themselves are created from old retired roads, upgraded, re-routed, or their number designations changed.

Many U.S. Forest Service trail number designations and names have been recently changed. In this guide I have titled the trails with the names and numbers that are currently being used by that agency on updated Forest Service maps and other literature. However, these names and numbers will not always agree with information on older trail signs. In the *Descriptions* of these trails I have tried to make reference to the names and numbers that I personally observed on current maps, other literature, or on trail signs.

In the *Trail Descriptions* section, I have made more detailed notes. This is a journal of trail features that I felt were important to note — viewpoints, trail junctions, vegetation, wildlife, and the approximate distance from the trail start to certain points along the trail. Distances are recorded to the nearest 0.1 miles.

The *Distances* noted within this section were obtained from pedometer readings to the nearest 0.1 mile. I make no claim that these mileages are exact. I have found, however, that they do compare well with distances calculated from topographic maps and those distances recorded on road and trail signs. They are relatively accurate and alert the traveller to location of significant trail features, junctions, viewpoints, or topography. The accuracy of a pedometer depends, of course, on how well the hiker has calculated a stride length for different trail conditions. I did, in fact, adjust stride length depending on whether I was climbing a steep or moderate slope or traveling on relatively level terrain.

If you own one, I would recommend that you use a pedometer in conjunction with this guide so that you can more easily relate your location to features mentioned in this guide.

The *Hiking times* listed should be considered as conservative, that is, longer than it would take most people to simply travel the trail. The times were based on my travel time including time to take notes, identify birds, eat lunch, scan an opposite slope with binoculars for feeding or bedded deer, and time to "smell the flowers."

Sources of Trail Information

Trail names and numbers. Most of the trails described in this guide lie at least partially within the administrative boundaries of the Prescott National Forest. Consequently, trail names and numbers that we have used in this guide are those assigned by that agency. In many cases these names or numbers appear on internal U.S. Forest Service documents but not on trail signs. Their existence, however, suggests that at some time, all trails maintained by the U.S. Forest Service, will eventually be correctly signed.

The more recently placed trail signs are thin fiberglass posts approximately 4 inches wide. The trail number will be oriented vertically and graphic decals will indicate the uses permitted on the trail. This same type of sign is used on unimproved roads, those considered suitable only for high-clearance vehicles such as pickups and 4-wheel drives. The road signs, though similar to the trail signs, will lack the use information.

Trail Profiles. The graphic profiles that accompany each trail description are accurate representations of elevational changes along a trail relative to distance traveled. They give the traveler a good idea of a trail's difficulty at least with respect to elevational change. Important features are also noted, giving the traveler a fair idea of distance traveled, particularly if a pedometer is not being used. These data were obtained by graphing elevation against distance for map points taken at incremental distances of 0.25 miles on 7.5 min. U.S.G.S. topographic maps. For short trails (less than 1 mi.) a map distance of 0.1 miles was used.

Maps. Plan your trip properly by using and carrying good maps with you. In the Prescott or Verde Valley areas, U.S.G.S. topographic quadrangles may be obtained from most outdoor suppliers and sporting goods dealers. Topgraphic and planimetric maps can also be ordered from the U.S. Forest Service. Special brochures and order forms are available at Ranger District and Supervisor's Offices. National Forest recreation maps (scale = 0.5 miles/inch) are generally available for purchase at these same offices.

The topographic maps do not always have hiking or riding trails marked on them. Although at a much smaller scale, the Forest Service maps, with these recreation features mapped, can be quite useful when used in conjunction with the topographic quadrangles. Carry both in the field. The outline maps presented in this trail guide are fairly accurate, but are really only intended as a guide to trail access points, features, and trail distances.

Abbreviations. There are a handful of abbreviations that I have used both in text and on maps throughout this guide.

> 4WD = Four wheel drive vehicle
> Deg. = Degrees (compass azimuth)
> FR = Forest Road
> Quad = U.S.G.S. topographic quadrangle
> TR = Trail
> U.S.G.S. = United States Geological Survey

Introduction

Why this guide?

The much visited and most spectacular areas of Arizona — Oak Creek Canyon, the Grand Canyon, and National Parks and Monuments generally have well-developed guides available to their trails. There is even an excellent guide to trails in the deserts and mountains bordering the Phoenix metro area.

The trails within the basins and mountains of central Arizona, however, are probably less well known and described. These trails have existed for decades as access routes to cattle watering devices, as ore hauling roads, or as logging roads. The burst of mining activity, particulary in the Bradshaw Mountains, in the late 1800s resulted in a network of roads and trails throughout that region, serving towns, homesteads, and mines. With the decline of hardrock mining in this region, these primitive roads fell into disuse. Many of them have now been officially closed to vehicular traffic by the responsible land management agencies and converted to recreational trails.

Hiking or Riding in the Mountains and Canyons of Central Arizona

Weather

It is sometimes difficult to dress for the weather in the mountains of central Arizona. With large elevation changes, the traveler can experience considerable variation in weather even on a single day. Trails that vary, for example, by over 3,000 feet in elevation can have temperature ranges from day to night of as much as 50-60 degrees on the same route during one 24-hour period. You need to plan for these variations by wearing layered clothing. In this way you can shed or add layers as needed for the moment.

Winter hiking and camping can be very comfortable and enjoyable; it can also be extremely dangerous to the unprepared. A day that starts out with sunshine and temperatures in the mid-fifties can turn within 24 hours to subfreezing with snow depths in excess of 12 inches. In winter always carry with you the minimum equipment and clothing that you might need to survive a night or two in the mountains.

Winter checklist. Most of the hikes or rides described herein can be traveled in one day, so I will not attempt to outline the checklist of supplies required of the serious backpacker. A day hike, nevertherless, can often turn into an overnight stay because of bad weather, injury, or a vehicular breakdown. For that reason I would recommend that each person carry at minimum the following: waterproof matches, fire starter, compass, small flashlight, space blanket, plastic raincoat, topo maps, high protein snack food, first-aid supplies, sunscreen, water purification tablets, and plenty of water. All of the foregoing will weigh only a couple of pounds but could save a life.

Summer has its own hazards. Temperatures during mid-summer often exceed 100 degrees F. at elevations below 5,000 feet. May and June are typically the hottest months at the highest elevations, July and August at lower elevations. From mid-July through September, hikers need to be cautious of afternoon thunderstorms. When storms are active in an area, stay off ridges, particularly when riding horseback. Avoid open areas and solitary trees. Seek heavily forested areas, caves, and lower slopes for protection.

Tending to be cool and dry, spring and fall are often the most pleasant seasons for hiking most of the central Arizona trails.

Make Your Trip a Safe One!

File a travel plan and don't hike alone! Never leave home without leaving enough information that someone can follow to find you: topographic maps with your route and destination, anticipated duration of the trip, traveling companions, and vehicle license and description.

When on the trail, be especially cautious on steep grades, loose rock, cliffs, and wet ground. Also during warm weather, be careful of your footing in places likely to conceal snakes. These situations can cause an uncontrolled fall or severe injury. Injuries normally considered minor can become life-threatening emergencies when they occur in remote country.

Always carry a fully equipped first-aid kit.

Water

Carry at least two quarts of water for a full day's hike or ride. In summer you may need about one gallon per person.

During the wet seasons, particularly late winter, many mountain washes will have running water. Don't trust it for drinking unless it is treated. Too many of these water sources have been contaminated by human waste, domestic livestock, or even by wildlife. Carry with you some water purification tablets and use them if necessary. The water sources least likely to be contaminated are bedrock springs and patches of snow.

Geology

The mountains and basins around Prescott lie within what is known to geologists as the Central Highland region. This broad area, oriented roughly in a NW-SE diagonal line, forms a transition zone between the lower deserts of the Basin and Range Province to the south and the Colorado Plateau to the northeast. This area has undergone much folding and faulting, finally being lifted higher than either the southern deserts or the broad Colorado Plateau.

Much of the mantle of these mountains, originating in the Paleozoic and Mesozoic eras, has been lost to the erosive power of water, wind, and freezing and thawing. What remains in much of this region is a core of the oldest rock on earth — hard igneous and metamorphic rock of the Precambrian age, possibly one to two billion years old.

The granites, gneisses, and schists typical of this region can also be seen in the deepest parts of the Grand Canyon's inner gorge. In the Prescott area, and more particularly at Granite Dells, can be seen the predominant rocks of the region — Precambrian granite that has been broken into blocks and rounded by weathering. The "spheroidal weathering" results when these rectangular blocks are attacked on all sides by the various physical forces, rounding these blocks at their vulnerable corners. It is this weathering of ancient granite that produces the typical coarse, angular gravels that overlay much of the land surface. Much of this "rotten granite" is lichen covered, adding splotches of grays, greens, and yellows to the surface of exposed rock.

The metamorphic rocks of this region are highly mineralized. The gold and silver bearing ores of the Bradshaw Mountains and the Sierra Prietas brought both fortune and fame to the region. Because of the need to protect the hard-rock mines and miners from raiding Apaches in the late 1800's, a military post was established at Fort Whipple, and eventually a townsite at Prescott. Mainly because of the importance of gold, the first Territorial Capitol was established at Prescott rather than at the much older settlement in Tucson.

It was copper, however, that became king. It was the mines around the town of Jerome, perched high on the east slopes of Mingus Mountain, that produced over $375 million in copper ore, before those mines finally closed in 1953. The remains of small copper mining operations can be seen along most of the trails throughout the Bradshaw Mountains, the Sierra Prietas, and on Mingus Mountain.

Ancient people of the region

Despite the generally semi-arid climate, lack of a substantial soil mantle or dependable water, there is ample evidence of a large prehistoric human population in this region. Many of the trails described herein pass through these areas of significant human habitation. The evidence can be seen as broken pottery shards, spear and arrow points, pit houses, and fortifications. These habitation sites, however, are extremely sensitive and easily damaged or destroyed.

These archaeological sites when they occur on public lands or Indian lands are protected by the Archaeological Resources Protection

Act of 1979. On State lands they are protected by the Arizona State Antiquities Act.

Many of the trails described in this guide pass near significant archaeological sites. The knowledge of their presence of course adds an element of mystery, historical interest to a trail hike or ride, and an increased sensitivity to our environment. We will not, however, give any information in these trail descriptions that would expose their locations. These sites are simply too sensitve to human use and abuse. I would suggest this, however — if the subject of archaeology interests you, do some reading and contact a local amateur archaeologist or archaeological society. Learn to recognize the subtle clues of human habitation that lie upon the land and the story that they tell. Then without disturbing sites or collecting artifacts, you can begin to unravel for yourself a fragment of the history of these ancient peoples.

There were probably over 4,000 people inhabitating the San Francisco Peaks area as well as areas to the south and west, including the Prescott area prior to A.D. 1064 when Sunset Crater erupted. They were believed to belong to the Sinagua (meaning "without water") culture. Those in the Prescott area belonged to a branch of this group and were called the Prescott culture and probably occupied houses in this area from about A.D. 1000 to A.D. 1200. By the year A.D. 1300, however, the entire population of this region had left, infiltering lands to the south and west, and being absorbed into tribes living in those areas.

The potshards and parts of vessels excavated from ruins in the Prescott area reveal a crude, uncomplicated ware. The shards, commonly referred to as "Prescott crud" came from vessels that were thick and coarse, with poorly applied and repetitive designs. The lack of craftmanship and artistry, unlike that of other southwestern prehistoric cultures, seems to indicate that the ceramic vessels of this culture were made for practical use only.

Vegetation

The mountain and plateau region of central Arizona is a vast expanse of rugged mountains, high elevation basins, grassland valleys, and deep canyons. This diverse topography has resulted in such diverse conditions of slope steepness, exposure, and elevational gradient so as to create a likewise diverse flora.

If you were to climb in a straight line from say Black Canyon City at an elevation of less than 3,000 feet to 8,000 feet at the top of Mt. Union in the northern Bradshaws, you would have traveled less than 30 miles. Yet, that elevational change of 5,000 feet will have produced changes in the biotic communities equivalent to traveling over 3,000 miles from the southern U.S. to Canada.

Since all of the trails described herein occur above 4,000 feet in elevation, I will confine the discussion to the major vegetation types that occur there. Keep in mind, however, that the vegetation that you see is not governed strictly by elevation. You will see, for example, scrub oaks typical of high desert country around Cordes Junction, occurring at 7,000 feet on the warm, dry south facing slopes of Mt. Tritle. On the other hand, quaking aspen, occurs at an elevation of 5,500 feet in the cool moist canyon of the Hassayampa River. You would normally expect it to occur at elevations of 8,000 feet or more.

The pinyon-juniper vegetation type is probably most typical of our region and is dominated by pinyon pine and two species of juniper (alligator juniper and Utah juniper). In the mountains around Prescott you may encounter some real alligator juniper giants with circumferences in excess of 20 feet. This vegetation zone will typically occur at elevations from 4,000 feet to about 6,500 feet where annual rainfall totals will vary between 10 and 20 inches.

As you move up in elevation you enter a transition zone with a whole mix of tree species. Ponderosa pines begin to occur at about 5,500 feet, but mixed with pinyons, junipers, and evergreen oaks (Arizona white oak and Emory oak). The warmer dryer south-facing slopes will have a mix of brush species such as mountain mahogany, cliffrose, California buckthorn, silktassel, Fendler ceanothus, and manzanita, in addition to the evergreen oaks.

Finally, at least in central Arizona, you reach elevations of up to 8,000 feet where you enter a so-called mixed conifer vegetation type. The most notable conifer species here is the beautiful white fir with its long bluish-green aromatic needles and its very symmetrical conical crown, everybody's idea of the perfect Christmas tree. It grows at these higher elevations in association with giant Douglas fir and ponderosa pine.

Slicing through the various vegetation zones are the ribbons of riparian vegetation that occur within the flood plains of permanent and temporary streams. The vegetation associations here consist largely of shrub and tree species whose roots must sit below the water table in order to survive. With dependable water, broad-leafed winter deciduous trees and shrubs provide the single most important habitat for wildlife in Arizona. As one travels one of these stream courses from low elevation to mountain top, there is a gradually changing composition to the vegetation. Cottonwoods, willows, boxelder, and walnuts occur within the lowest warmest sites with a gradual transition to ashes, alders, and maples at the higher elevations. There are also two notable trees species that, while deciduous, are not limited to stream channels. These are the Gambel oak, locally abundant throughout this region, and quaking aspen.

14

Wildlife

With such a diversity of vegetation you would expect a likewise diverse fauna. It is in fact so diverse that it defies cataloging at least within a book not devoted exclusively to that purpose. A few of the more notable species are worth mentioning, however. Since most hiking and horseback riding is done during daylight hours, one is less likely to see the many mammalian species that are most active at night or during the hours before dawn and after sunset. Nevertheless, with a good pair of binoculars, some patience, and some awareness of the likely habitat of a species, one can be richly rewarded with the sight of a bedded deer, a herd of javelina feeding along a warm hillside, or a tassel-eared squirrel clipping pine scales overhead. The black bear is often seen in fall along lower slopes, harvesting the fruit of the prickly pear cactus. More often they stay secluded in the deep cool canyons and dense riparian habitat. Mountain lions, with their extensive home areas, are seldom seen but always present somewhere within any mountain range. Javelina, typically a desert species, are expanding their range throughout Arizona and seem to be adapting unexpectedly to some of the colder conifer-covered mountains. Coyotes, bobcats, and foxes are common and their tracks can almost always be seen along stretches of mountain trails.

In fact, to add another dimension to your hike, take along a guide to the tracks of mammals and birds. I say birds because wild turkeys also hike our mountain trails for short distances and are commonly seen close to forest edge residential developments in the Prescott area.

The avian species likely to be present along a particular trail are too numerous to catalog. Their presence depends on time of year, time of day, and habitat type. I have made a few scattered notes about birds that I have seen along particular trails, but these represent only a sampling of what is there. If bird identification turns you on, take written notes on the characteristics of birds you can't identify; then refer to your bird guide when you get home.

Bradshaw Mountains

THIS HEAVILY FORESTED AND RUGGED NORTH-SOUTH ORIENTED RANGE is a major topographic feature of central Arizona. The area was named for William Bradshaw, a miner who followed the Walker party to Arizona in the 1860s. Towers Mountain dominates the landscape in the south and Mount Union in the Walker area, the latter peak rising to almost 8,000 feet in elevation. Because of their north-south orientation, the highest elevations tend to collect some of the heaviest rainfall in the state. Single storm totals sometimes exceed 10 inches.

Though there are few permanent streams, these mountains give their seasonal flows to two south-flowing rivers, the Agua Fria on the east, and the Hassayampa to the west.

Despite being completely within the administrative boundaries of the Prescott National Forest, both seasonal and permanent residences are scattered throughout the Bradshaws. There is a good reason for the many so-called forest "in-holdings" — gold! These mountains were so extensively mined for gold from the late 1800s to the present that there seems hardly a road or trail in the entire area that doesn't pass their remains. Many of these mining properties were subsequently patented and ultimately sold as residential parcels.

Though placer and hard rock mines have left an indelible mark on the natural environment, they are also a part of the rich historical heritage of this region.

As you travel the trails through this remote and severely dissected mountain range you can only marvel at the tenacity, ingenuity, and

Palace Station

perseverance of the miners, explorers, and military that first opened the region to industry and settlement. Contemplating these events of the past adds another dimension to the pleasure of hiking and riding in these mountains.

BANNING CREEK TRAIL

General information:
For a pleasant and varied hike in the northern Bradshaws, try this route between the Hidden Valley Ranch residential area and Goldwater Lake.

In the spring, because the route follows a perennial stream, you will encounter a variety of flowers and water-loving plants, deep pools, and small waterfalls.

In the fall the deciduous trees that take their moisture from this wet creek bottom turn to various shades of yellow and orange. Very old apple trees of at least two varieties may be laden with apples in some years.

Another fruit that may occur in abundance in some years is the canyon grape. During my last trip to this area, the party I was with collected about 6 pounds of grapes, which I made into jelly and syrup.

Access and trailhead location: **Map: p. 19**
There are a couple of approaches to Banning Creek and the trail along it. One is from the south end of Cougar Trail, a private road at the southeastern extremity of the Hidden Valley Ranch residential subdivision. Because many roads within this subdivision are private, there is no legal public access at this point.

Banning Creek can also be reached in a 20 minute walk from the White Spar Campground on Highway 89. Drive south from downtown Prescott on Montezuma Street for 3.0 miles. Turn left into the entrance to the White Spar Campground. At the fork just a few yards from Highway 89, drive left into the campground. Continue straight north through the campground area to a sign that reads: *"Reservation Area Campsites, 46-63."* Turn right here. Within just a few yards you will come to a small brown shed on the left of the road. The trail to Banning Creek leaves to the east just a few feet south of this building.

Road condition: Paved.

Hiking time: 1.5 hours.

Length: 2.8 miles from White Spar Campground to Goldwater Lake.

Difficulty: Moderate.   *Use:* Moderate.

Uses permitted: Hiking, bicycling, and horseback riding only.

Recommended seasons of use: Spring, fall, winter.

Maps, other resources: Prescott National Forest, west half; U.S.G.S. topographic 7.5' quads for Prescott and Groom Creek.

Trail description:

The trail from White Spar Campground heads east and climbs fairly steeply for about 0.2 miles. Though not maintained, it is easy to follow. At 0.3 miles the route contours around the north end of a forested knoll. At 0.4 miles, be alert. Within a shallow drainage that the trail is following, another trail leaves to the left. Stay right.

At 0.5 miles, where the trail is descending a shallow wash, you will encounter some rocks lined across the drainage. The trail goes sharply right here and then merges with a trail coming in from the left.

At 0.8 miles the trail reaches Banning Creek at the site of the apple and pear orchard. At this point a left fork crosses over the creek to FR 61 and the access gate to the residential area. The right fork goes south along the west side of the creek. Following the west-side trail, you will pass big cottonwood, boxelder, willow, and walnut trees.

At mile 1.7, FR 9403S turns right and joins the Schoolhouse Gulch in 0.7 miles. From there it is another 0.7 miles back to the White Spar Campground. Thus, a round-trip starting at the campground, but using FR 9403S and the Schoolhouse Gulch road (FR 62) as a return route, would be 3.1 miles.

If you continue south along FR 61, the road forks again at mile 1.8. The right fork goes through an open meadow bordered with tall Lombardy poplars and, within a few yards, ends at a small pool. Here the stream cascades over dark metamorphic rocks. Canyon grape vines cover the boulders above the pool.

The left fork of the road continues to Goldwater Lake. At mile 2.1 there is a padlocked aluminum gate. City of Prescott officials, however, assured me that they had no objections to hikers or mountain bike riders continuing to Goldwater Lake, **if they stay on the road.** People are strictly prohibited from crossing fence lines in the vicinity of the dams on the two lakes.

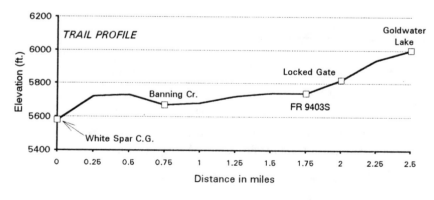

BANNING CREEK TRAIL

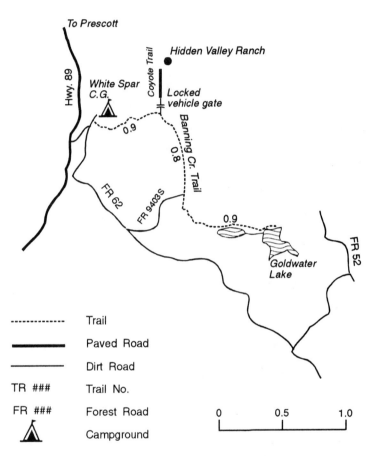

- - - - - - - -	Trail
▬▬▬▬▬	Paved Road
───────	Dirt Road
TR ###	Trail No.
FR ###	Forest Road
⛺	Campground

0   0.5   1.0

BOY SCOUT TRAIL #126

General information:

This canyon trail connects the Ranch Trail #62 in the north end of the Bradshaw Mountains and Government Canyon to the west. Although quite short, it provides access to other trails in the northern Bradshaw Mountains. Access to the west end of the trail is through State Trust Land. Only recently, the Yavapai Trails Association succeeded in obtaining a Heritage Fund Grant. They applied some of that award to the purchase of a right-of-way through the state land, thus providing legal access to Government Canyon north of Oak Knoll Village and Trail #126.

Access and trailhead location: Map: p. 31

To reach the east end of the trail you must first travel on Trail #299 and Trail #62. From downtown Prescott drive east on Gurley St. to Mt. Vernon St. (Senator Highway) then south for approximately 4.1 miles. The trailhead sign for Trail #299 is on the east side of the road just past Goldwater Lake and about 0.9 miles before the turnoff to the Spruce Mountain Road (FR 52A). The upper trailhead is located on the left side of the Spruce Mountain Road (FR 52A) 1.5 miles from the Senator Highway. Travel up Trail #299 (Watershed Trail) for 3.1 miles to its junction with Trail #62. Go north on Trail #62 for 1.2 miles to the junction with Trail #126. Though the junction is easily recognized, there is no sign to mark it.

To reach the west end of the trail, travel only 2.5 miles south on the Senator Highway from Gurley St. in Prescott to Sweet Acres Drive. Go east on this road for about 0.3 miles to the Pine Ridge Dr. loop road. Stay left here for another 0.2 miles to a point just beyond where the road crosses Government Canyon. On the left you will see a 4WD road going north and a State Trust Land sign on a tree to the right of this road. Park here.

Road condition: Paved on Senator Highway. FR 52A is dirt but suitable for all vehicles when dry and snow-free.

Hiking time: 1.5 hours.   *Length:* 2.1 mile.

Difficulty: Easy.   *Use:* Light.

Uses permitted: Hiking, horseback riding, and cycling. The trail follows a rocky wash in a number of places making it unsuitable for bicycles.

Recommended seasons of use: spring, summer, fall

Maps, other resources: Prescott National Forest, west half; U.S.G.S. topographic 7.5' quads for Prescott and Groom Creek.

Trail description:

From the junction with Trail #62, Trail #126 heads in a north-northwest direction staying just to the north of a small drainage. Though indistinct, it is not too hard to follow if you are careful to look ahead for the trail direction.

At mile 0.4 the trail passes an old spring box, then climbs away from and to the south of the wash climbing over a small knoll.

At mile 0.5 there is no trail, just a jumble of wash bottom trees and shrubs. There is well-developed riparian vegetation in places along here — mature shrub willows, walnut trees, wild grape, and ash.

At 0.7 miles the trail has disappeared again. You have to pick your way through rocks and brush. It is a scenic area, made so by the cascading creek as it passes over dark rock shelves. Just beyond here be alert to where the trail leaves to the north of the creek. The trail, though narrow, is now easy to follow as it passes through thick brush.

At 0.8 miles and well above the wash, you finally get some views of Thumb Butte and the ridge of the Sierra Prieta to the west.

At 0.9 miles a Forest Service gate crosses the trail.

At mile 1.2, after passing a mine, the trail merges with a 4WD road. Following this road to the left will eventually lead you to a large clearing. This was a habitation site once as indicated by ruins of buildings and some cultivated fruit trees. A large pear tree just to the right of the trail was laden with small pears. A mass of tiny yellow flowers covered the ground here. I identified these as *Viguiera multiflora*, a small composite commonly called showy goldeneye.

At 1.45 miles where the trail reenters the pine forest, the road forks. The right fork goes into and then north along Government Canyon. The left fork goes to the Oak Knoll Village residential area. The trail in this area passes through an open park-like ponderosa pine forest.

At mile 2.1 the trail exits onto Pine Ridge Drive.

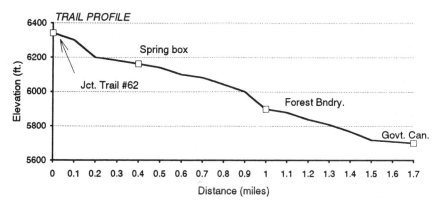

GROOM CREEK LOOP TRAIL #307

General information:

This is one of the most attractive trails in the entire trail system on the Prescott National Forest, particularly for horseback riders. This is in part due to the construction of a Horse Camp just south of Groom Creek. A very scenic trail, it passes through attractive stands of Ponderosa pine. On Spruce Ridge, where trees do not obstruct the view, you can get panoramic views of the Crown King area, Prescott area, Mingus, and on a clear day, the San Francisco Peaks. The ride or hike up the Wolf Creek drainage to Spruce Mountain is particularly attractive.

Also, at the Spruce Mountain Lookout area, look for this unusual natural phenomenon: in summer, swarms of ladybugs (more correctly ladybeetles) blanket trees, bushes, and rocks in concentrations exceeding 120 million per acre on the higher peaks of the Bradshaws and Sierra Prietas. Although they can be gathered by the quart, don't bother taking them home. The ladybugs at this time of year are in a period of estivation (dormancy), neither feeding nor mating, and will not feed on your garden insects.

This is a well-maintained trail, and its excellent condition makes it one of the best in the system. Because this trail loops back to the Horse Camp, it makes the 9-mile loop a feasible distance to do in one day either on horseback or on foot.

Access and trailhead location: Map p. 31

The Groom Creek Horse Camp is approximately 6.5 miles south of Prescott on the Senator Highway (FR 52). Hikers may also reach the trail from the top of Spruce Mountain where there is a maintained picnic area. To find the trail at this point, first drive east on Gurley St. from downtown Prescott to Mount Vernon St. Turn right (south). This road becomes the Senator Highway and, once within the Prescott National Forest, becomes Forest Road 52. Continue south from Gurley St. for approximately 4.5 miles to Forest Road 52A (on east side of main road). You will have just passed the entrance to Goldwater Lake before coming to FR 52A. Turn left onto FR 52A and travel for about 4 miles to the picnic area.

Road condition: Paved on FR 52 to Groom Creek, then unpaved to the picnic area

Hiking time: 6 hours   *Length:* 8.7 miles

Difficulty: Difficult if hiking, depending on direction of travel.

Use: Heavy

Uses permitted: Hiking, horseback riding, bicycling (non-motorized).

Recommended seasons of use: Spring, summer (if horseback), fall.

Maps, other resources: Prescott National Forest, west half; U.S.G.S. topographic 7.5' quads for Groom Creek.

Trail description:

From the north loop at the Horse Camp, the trail stays almost entirely in timber. It climbs for about 2.8 miles through the upper Wolf Creek drainage to the top of Spruce Mountain. At mile 1.5 a sign directs you 1.2 miles farther to the Spruce Mtn. fire lookout. It also points to a trail going southeast to the Transcendent Mine Road. This side trail climbs steadily for about 640 feet in 0.8 miles to the South Spruce Ridge.

From the Spruce Mountain Lookout, the trail turns southwest down the South Spruce Ridge. At 1.5 miles you will encounter a trail sign at the southern end of the unnumbered trail connecting to the north loop. Continuing for 0.3 miles farther, you will encounter a sign on your right showing the direction to the South Spruce Ridge Heliport. Then 0.2 miles farther, there is a sign for Trail #77 (Isabella Trail) which goes south to Potato Patch, a distance of 1.0 miles. From here it is another 5.4 miles on Trail #307 to the Senator Road (FR 52).

If you travel Trail #77, you will find another sign within about 50 feet. It shows a distance of 1.0 miles to the Transcendent Mine Rd. and 2 miles to the Senator Road. You will come to the mine road in about 15 minutes. Take the road to the right to reach the Walker Road (FR 197). From here turn right to Hassayampa Lake and the Senator Highway and left to Potato Patch. The trail sign at the Walker Road shows that the Isabella Trail is #67 rather than #77 as indicated where the trail connects with Trail #307. The #77 is probably correct.

Tip!

For a shorter round-trip than the complete loop on Trail #307, consider using the unnumbered connector trail between the loops that is described above. This would result in a round-trip of about 7 miles, rather than the 9 miles required to complete Trail #307.

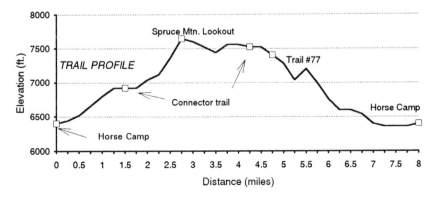

THE RANCH TRAIL #62

General information:

This trail connects Watershed Trail #299 and the road to Walker. The particular attraction of this trail, besides the fact that it is easy to follow and well maintained, is in the cross-section of country that it traverses. From its junction with Trail #299 to the trailhead on the Walker Road, the trail descends an elevation gradient of almost 1,200 feet. In so doing it passes through most of the vegetation types represented in the Prescott area.

Toward the northern end of the trail there are broad views to the north of Glassford Hill, the Prescott Valley area, Bill Williams Mtn. and the San Francisco Peaks. At the upper end of the trail the views are more restricted since the trail stays within pine forest. There are, however, some nice views to the east of the Lynx Lake area.

Depending on time of year and time of day, one could expect to see a variety of wildlife species. Mule deer, black bear, tassel-eared (Aberts) squirrels, and wild turkeys would most likely be seen (at least their tracks) at upper elevations, with signs of javelina somewhat lower.

Access to trailhead location: Map p. 31

Drive east from downtown Prescott on Highway 69 to just past the residential development "The Ranch at Prescott." Drive south at the sign to Lynx Lake (Walker Rd.) and go just 0.5 miles to a large parking area and trailhead on the west side of the road.

This trail climbs an elevation gradient of almost 1,200 feet from the trailhead at the Walker Rd. With this in mind, hikers might consider hiking from the top down. Access here is via Trail #299. Drive east on Gurley St. from downtown Prescott to Mt. Vernon Street (Senator Highway). Turn right and go south for approximately 4.1 miles. The trailhead sign is on the east side of the road just past Goldwater Lake and about 0.9 miles before the turnoff to Spruce Mountain Road (FR 52A). From here hike or ride Trail #299 for 1.4 miles to where it intersects Trail #62.

Road Condition: Paved to the north trailhead and paved on the Senator Highway to reach the trail via Trail #299

Length: 4.8 miles

Difficulty: Moderate, depending on direction of travel

Use: Moderate

Uses permitted: Hiking, horseback riding, bicycles (non-motorized)

Recommended seasons of use: Spring, fall, summer (hot), early winter

Maps, other resources: Prescott National Forest, west half; U.S.G.S. topographic 7.5' quads for Prescott and Groom Creek.

Trail description:

From its junction with Trail #299, this trail goes north through tall ponderosa pines. Being in pine and Gambel oak, the trail is padded with fallen leaves and pine needles for the first mile or so.

At mile 1.2 the trail begins a steep descent into a small drainage that feeds into Government Canyon to the west. As you reach this drainage you will encounter a sign for Trail #126. This latter trail goes north-northwest down this drainage and eventually joins the trails along Government Canyon. Trail #126 reaches the Prescott National Forest boundary within 1 mile. This route is described elsewhere in this guide.

At about mile 2.0, Trail #62 climbs a high knoll to about 6,400 feet. This hill is mainly brush covered and affords some grand views in all directions. The trail stays along this high ridge for about another 0.5 miles and then begins a steady descent of over 1,000 feet in the remaining 2 miles.

At mile 4.2 you will encounter a hinged metal gate. Be sure to close this gate after passing. Then within another 0.4 miles there is a rock cairn to indicate direction to Trail #62. As you reach the lower end of this trail, passing just to the east of the residential development, many heavily used local trails begin to intersect. Watch carefully for the direction of the main trail out to the Walker Road. You will reach this roadside trailhead at approximately 4.8 miles.

Tip!

For a pleasant downhill hike, use two vehicles. Leave one at the Walker Road trailhead and take the second to the trailhead for Trail #299 on the Senator Hwy. The hike up Trail #299 is steep for 1.3 miles to its junction with Trail #62, but then it's almost all downhill to the Walker Road trailhead. This would make a total trip of about 6 miles.

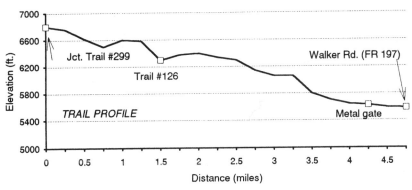

SMITH RAVINE TRAIL #297

General information:

This rather short trail (1.7 miles) climbs through an attractive canyon — Smith Ravine. It travels under an almost continuous forest canopy of ponderosa pine and Gambel oaks, and consequently, has few good viewpoints. Although we hiked the trail in December of 1993 when the deciduous trees were leafless, I expect that this canyon is especially lovely in the spring when the broadleaf trees are again fully leafed.

The trail connects between the Spruce Mountain Road (FR 52A) and the Walker Road (FR 197) via FR 25. Though fairly short itself, this trail is close enough to the trails in the vicinity of Spruce Mountain to provide much longer hikes or rides that connect between the Walker Road and the Senator Highway (see *Tips* below).

Access and trailhead location: Map: p. 31

To reach the east trailhead first drive east on Gurley Street from downtown Prescott. Then take Highway 69 east to the traffic light at the Walker Road junction, a distance from downtown Prescott of 4.2 miles. Turn right (south) and drive an additional 4.9 miles to the well-marked junction with the Smith Ravine Road (FR 25). Turn right here (west) and drive another 1.0 miles along this dirt road to a locked gate. There is ample room here to park off the road. The "Private Property" sign here is rather intimidating, though is intended to discourage vehicular traffic. The trail junction, however, is another 0.6 miles farther up this road. The dilemma for the hiker is that there is also nothing to indicate just where the private portion of the road ends and public land begins. My advice is to simply skirt the private property by hiking to the east of Smith Ravine, staying close to the canyon itself. The trailhead is on the old road, but 0.6 miles beyond the gate.

The Forest Service plans to extend this trail to the Walker Road, bypassing the private property.

Another approach to this trail is from the Spruce Mountain Road (FR 52A). From downtown Prescott drive east to Mt. Vernon St. and then turn right (south). This road becomes the Senator Highway and, once within the Prescott National Forest, becomes Forest Road 52. Continue south on FR 52 for approximately 4.5 miles to Forest Road 52A (on east side of main road). If you come to Marapai Road on your right, you will have gone about 0.1 miles past the FR 52A turnoff. Turn left onto FR 52A and travel for approximately 2.6 miles to the trailhead for Trail #297. You will have passed the trailhead for Trail #299 at 1.4 miles after leaving the Senator Highway. The trail sign for Trail #297 is not clearly visible from FR 52A. What marks this spot, however, is a secondary road that leaves FR 52A at this point to the east and passes through a wide gate comprised of two tall posts with a guy wire across the top of the posts. The trailhead sign is right at this gate and within a few yards of the Spruce Mountain Road.

Road condition: FR 52A is suitable for all vehicles; FR 25 is suitable for high-clearance vehicles if dry and free of snow.

Hiking time: 1 hour   *Length:* 1.8 miles

Difficulty: Easy   *Use:* Light.

Uses permitted: Hiking, horseback riding, and bicycling (including motorized).

Recommended season of use: spring, summer, fall

Maps, other resources: Prescott National Forest, west half; U.S.G.S. topographic 7.5' quad for Groom Creek.

Trail description:

Since I traveled this trail from FR 25 to the Spruce Mountain Road, I will describe it in the same direction. The last residence on FR 25 is 0.5 miles west of the private property gate. The trailhead sign is 0.6 miles from the gate.

At mile 0.1 miles from the trailhead there is a critical trail junction. One trail continues up Smith Ravine; Trail #297 turn sharply right (west). as indicated by a small redwood trail sign.

At mile 0.5, after a fairly steep climb, the trail reaches a saddle and then descends gradually to the west. The lower part of the trail was snow-covered when we last hiked it. The upper parts, however, were not and revealed a smooth well maintained surface. With the exception of a few spots on the lower trail, I think it is quite suitable for bicycles.

At 1.5 miles the trail breaks out of the timbered ravine and approaches a saddle across an open south facing slope. This slope is covered with mostly manzanita and alligator juniper. As you near this saddle you will get your first glimpse of the fire lookout tower atop Spruce Mountain.

At 1.7 miles the trail ends on the Spruce Mountain Road (FR 52A. This junction is marked with a fiberglass trail sign. The sign shows permitted uses to include motorcycles, contrary to what is indicated on the sign at the east end. The Forest Service, confirmed, however, that for now at least, motorized cycles are permitted.

Tip!

Trail #297 can be conveniently combined with Trail #299 or Trail #307 for a much longer hike or ride. From the point where Trail #297 meets the Spruce Mountain Road, it is just 1.2 miles north on this road to the upper trailhead for Trail #299 (the Watershed Trail). A trip along this route from the Walker Road to the Senator Highway would comprise about 6.4 miles.

Trail #297 can also be combined with Trail #307. The Spruce Mountain lookout tower and picnic area is just 1.4 miles south of the point where Trail #297 meets FR 52A. A trip up Trail #297, south along FR 52A, and then west along the north leg of Trail #307 to the Senator Highway would also be about 6.4 miles.

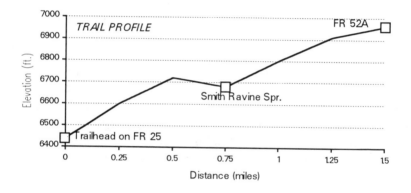

WATERSHED TRAIL #299

General information:

This trail, in the Groom Creek area, offers a moderately easy day hike or ride to a ridge east of upper Goldwater Lake. The lower elevation portions of this trail go through a dense mix of scrub oak, mountain mahogany, juniper and pinyon pine. As the trail ascends, it moves into stands of ponderosa pine and Gambel oak. The visibility from the ridge above Goldwater Lake allows a 360 degree view of much of northern Arizona. The trail name comes from the fact that the ridge that it occupies divides two major drainages: Banning Creek to the west to Goldwater Lake, and Sawmill Gulch to the east, and other drainages feeding into Lynx Creek and eventually Lynx Lake.

Access to trailhead location:

From Prescott drive south on the Mt. Vernon Street (Senator Highway) for approximately 4.1 miles. The trailhead sign is on the east side of the road just past Goldwater Lake. You will find the upper trailhead on the left side of the Spruce Mountain Road (FR 52A) 1.5 miles from the Senator Highway.

Road Condition: The Senator Highway is paved as far as Groom Creek. The Spruce Mountain Road (FR 52A) is dirt, but suitable for all vehicles when the road surface is dry.

Hiking Time: 2 hours   *Length:* 2.8 miles

Difficulty: Moderate   *Use:* Heavy

Uses permitted: Hiking, horseback riding, bicycles, motorcycles.

Recommended seasons of use: Spring, fall, summer (hot), early winter.

Maps, other resources: Prescott National Forest, west half; U.S.G.S. topographic 7.5' quad for Groom Creek.

Trail description: Map p. 31

The trail leaves the Senator Highway at an elevation of about 6,200 ft. climbing steeply to Deer Lick Spring. The lower portion of this trail stays in dense stands of scrub oak, mountain mahogany, juniper, and pinyon pine. Hikers descending to the west on the trail need to be careful of their footing because of the loose rock and steep grade. At mile 0.5 there is a clear view to the south of Maverick Mtn. and Mt. Tritle. At 0.7 miles you will pass through a wire gate and enter an attractive park-like ponderosa pine stand.

At 1 mile from the start, you will reach Deer Lick Spring. Water may be available for horses in a concrete trough located on the south side of the trail. Within a quarter-mile past the spring you will reach an old, routed-wood trail sign showing distances and directions to an old BSA Trail and to the Spruce Mtn. Road (FR 52A). The trail then passes under a transmission line and at 1.3 miles reaches a trail junction.

The trail going northeast from here is the upper (southern) end of the Ranch Trail (Trail #62). Watershed Trail turns southeast from here climbing to the top of the ridge reaching an elevation of 6,840 ft. There is a clear view from here of Bigelow Peak almost due east of the trail.

After reaching its highest point, the trail heads almost due south for 0.8 miles to where it intersects FR 52A (Spruce Mtn. lookout road). Before reaching the road, the trail will pass beneath the transmission line several times. Be careful at these junctions to stay on the main trail. The trails following the transmission line have posts planted across them to deny access to anything larger than a motorcycle and to also avoid confusing these trails with the Watershed Trail.

Within 100 yards of the Spruce Mtn. Road, the trail forks. The right fork (south) goes a short distance to a grand overlook. From this point one can gain a 360 degree panorama of northern Arizona. To the north lies the often snow-capped San Francisco peaks, with Bill Williams Mountain to the west. To the northwest Granite Mountain dominates the near landscape. Mt. Tritle and Maverick Mountain lie to the southwest, and Spruce Mountain to the southeast. Returning to and continuing on the main trail, you will reach the Spruce Mtn. road within 100 yards.

Tip!
To travel the 2.8 miles of this trail one-way and downhill, use two vehicles. Park one at the upper trailhead on the Spruce Mtn. road (FR 52A) and the other on the Senator Highway at the lower trailhead. A round-trip by vehicle between these two points requires only about 30 minutes.

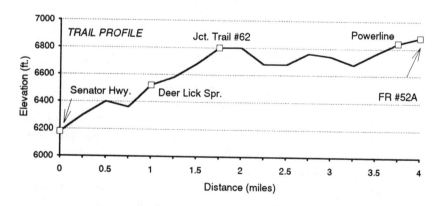

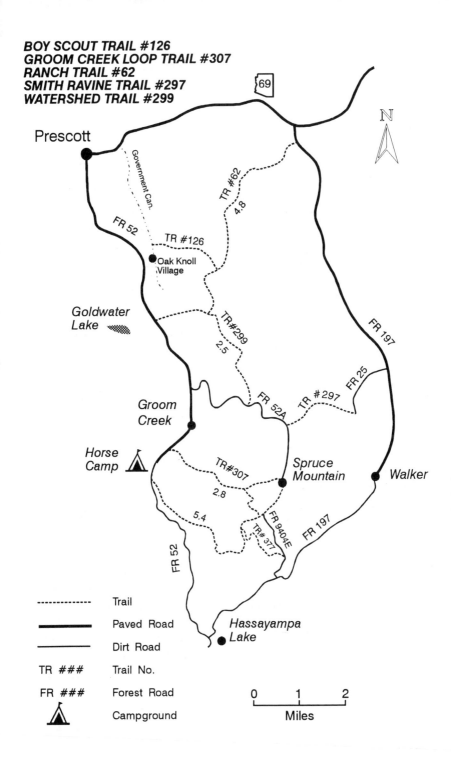

BOY SCOUT TRAIL #126
GROOM CREEK LOOP TRAIL #307
RANCH TRAIL #62
SMITH RAVINE TRAIL #297
WATERSHED TRAIL #299

69

N

Prescott

Government Can.

TR #62
4.8

FR 52

TR #126

Oak Knoll
Village

Goldwater
Lake

TR #299
2.5

FR 197

Groom
Creek

FR 52A

TR #297

FR 25

Horse
Camp

TR #307
2.8

Spruce
Mountain

Walker

5.4

FR 9404E

TR# 377

FR 197

FR 52

Hassayampa
Lake

- - - - - - Trail

━━━━━ Paved Road

───── Dirt Road

TR ###   Trail No.

FR ###   Forest Road

Campground

0   1   2
Miles

E CROSS L TRAIL #281

General information:

There are no great vistas from this trail, so it should be enjoyed for its more intimate features. This is, however, one of the most soul-satisfying routes of all that I have traveled. A live stream springing from the southern flank of Lookout Mountain parallels the route for much of its length. Water works its magic as it tumbles over shelves of metamorphic rock, creating pools lined with yellow monkey flowers and columbine. A forest canopy of ponderosa pines, Gambel oaks, and scattered white firs provides almost continuous shade along this route.

If a flash of brilliant tomato-red catches your glance, it is likely a painted redstart, an energetic and very conspicuous wood warbler that frequents stretches of this riparian woodland. Its black hood, red breast, and broad white wing bar make it hard to misidentify.

Miners and ranchers have also found this Ash Creek area attractive as confirmed by the many stone walls, building foundations, rusting equipment, and collapsing cabins that line the creek.

So it was in the early summer of 1993 following an unusually wet winter. Ash Creek, however, in periods of drought is likely to be dry, with only remnant pools scattered along its length. So, do not depend on it for drinking water, and if you do use it, be sure to purify it.

Travelers on this trail should plan enough time to visit the old Palace Station. It is now a Forest Service administrative and information site. It served until about 1910 as a stage stop at Spence Spring, about halfway on the route between Prescott and Crown King.

Access and trailhead location: Map: p. 41

The northern access to the trail is probably preferable, particularly for hikers, since it is the highest elevation along the trail. Take the Senator Highway (FR 52) south from Prescott for approximately 11 miles to the turnoff to Mt. Union (FR 261). Continue south on FR 52 for 0.3 miles to FR 52B. Take FR 52B west for 0.3 miles to its junction with FR 81. Take FR 81 south for another 0.3 miles to the junction with FR 70. Park your vehicle somewhere in this vicinity. Then walk or ride southeast along the Ash Creek Ridge for about 0.4 miles to the trailhead sign.

Road condition: FR 52B and FR 81 are suitable for high clearance vehicles. FR 70, however, is very rough in spots and is for 4WD vehicles only.

Hiking time: 6 hours   *Length:* 6.5 miles

Difficulty: Moderately difficult, mainly because of the steep climb to the Ash Creek Ridge.   *Use:* Light

Uses permitted: Hiking, horseback riding, and bicycling .

Recommended season of use: spring, summer, fall

Maps, other resources: Prescott National Forest, west half; U.S.G.S. topographic 7.5′ quads for Battleship Butte and Groom Creek.

Precaution: The danger of forest fire becomes particularly acute in the remoteness of the Ash Creek drainage. Fire in deep canyons such as this are tough to spot and tougher to approach and fight. Never build an open fire when camping in this country.

Trail description:

The initial half-mile along FR 70 to the well-marked trailhead is a pleasant walk under a mixed conifer canopy of Douglas firs and ponderosa pines, and Gambel oaks. The upper part of the trail as it descends to the Ash Creek drainage, contours around the southeast side of Lookout Mountain .

At 1.2 miles (from FR 81) the trail reaches Ash Creek. Groves of Arizona walnut, box elder, and ash trees line this drainage. If the creek is flowing, you should see pockets of yellow columbine. It likes the damp rich soils of creek banks. With a liking for even wetter sites, the yellow monkeyflower will be seen lining the little pools all along Ash Creek.

About one-half mile below this junction a pipeline runs parallel to the creek along the west bank. This pipe carries water from the creek to the crumbling cabin and barn below and was originally used for irrigation. This pipe lies on part of a 6-acre private parcel of land which surrounds the two wooden buildings. Please respect private property rights here by staying on the main trail on the east side of the creek.

A well-marked trail junction is located at mile 3.3. The main trail turns sharply east from here by way of a small drainage to the Ash Creek Ridge and eventually the Senator Highway (FR 52). A spur trail for Trail #281 continues along Ash Creek for another 0.4 miles to its junction with FR 82.

For the first 100 yards the climb to the ridge is quite steep. Within just a short distance you will encounter what appears to have been a home site. Only a concrete foundation, a rusty cook-stove, barrels, and machinery parts remain. A miner is reported to have lived here as late as the 1950's.

Columbine

After traveling about 4.3 miles from FR 81 you will reach the steepest part of this trail as it goes through a series of severe switchbacks, finally reaching the Ash Creek Ridge at mile 4.7. Here FR 70 goes both north and south along the ridge. Trail #381 (#81) leaves directly across this road, going in a northeast direction for 1.5 miles to FR 52.

To continue on Trail #281, turn south on FR 70 at the ridge junction and go for about 25 yards to the well-marked trail junction. Trail #281 heads east from here for 1.5 miles to FR 52. It follows a shaded but dry canyon through stands of pine and Gambel oak. If the abundant New Mexico locust is blooming along here it can be spectacular.

After a total of just over 6 miles you will reach FR 52 a few hundred yards north of Palace Station.

Tip!

For a round-trip of about 5.6 miles, follow Trail #281 as outlined above. But, instead of going to Palace Station, turn north on FR 70 at the Ash Creek Ridge junction. Travel for 2.1 miles back to your vehicle at the junction of FR 70 and FR 81. To avoid the steep climb to the Ash Creek Ridge, you might consider reversing the direction of travel. Descend the steep switchbacks to Ash Creek; then travel north along Ash Creek, returning to the ridge on the more gentle contours of the northern portion of Trail #281.

For a round-trip of about 10 miles, begin the trip at the Palace Station trailhead. Follow Trail #281 west to Ash Creek, then north to FR 70. Then go south on FR 70 along the Ash Creek Ridge to the junction with Trail #281. Then return to the start along the 1.5-mile section of Trail #281 that you started on.

For a 5 mile bicycle route, go west on Trail #281 from Palace Station to the Ash Creek Ridge. Then go north on FR 70 for just a few yards to the trail junction with Trail #81. Go northeast on Trail #81 to FR 52, then south on this road to Palace Station.

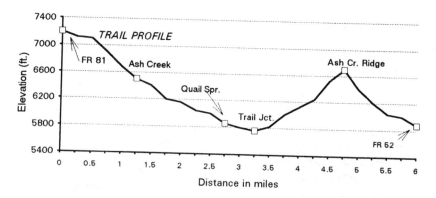

VENEZIA TRAIL #381 (#81)

General information:

I have given the above name to this trail because of its proximity to the site of the Venezia mine and townsite.

A Post Office was established in this vicinity in 1916 and discontinued in June of 1935. At one time the town actually numbered 73 citizens. The village businesses included a merchandise store and a stage line to Crown King. The name of the village is credited to F. Scopel, a local settler and Italian immigrant, who apparently named the site for his native Venice. All that remains today are stone building foundations located just a few hundred yards north of the trailhead and adjacent to the roadway.

The mine, with extensive vertical and horizontal shafts, is located in a fissure of the Mt. Union claims and, in the early 1900's, was one of the best producers of "free gold" in the vicinity. The concrete platforms and pilings are all that remains of a 20-stamp mill erected on the site in 1910 to process these ores.

The trail connects Senator Highway in Crooks Canyon and the Ash Creek Ridge. From the east trailhead it climbs gradually along the southeast flank of Ash Creek Ridge for about 1.8 miles and gains about 560 feet in altitude. There it meets the 4WD road on the ridge and Trail #281.

Besides the on-site qualities of the trail, the Venezia Trail offers a connecting link between several other roads and trails. Cyclists (non-motorized) could, for example, come up the Venezia Trail, turn south along the Ash Creek Ridge road for 0.25 miles, then travel east for another mile to Palace Station along the east leg of Trail #281. Then the distance back to your starting point would then be another 1.4 miles. Since the Venezia Trail allows motorcycles, it could be traveled in combination with the road north along Ash Creek and comprise a much longer round-trip.

The trail goes through a woodland of ponderosa pines, and Gambel and evergreen oaks. The forest canopy provides plenty of shade and a pleasant hike even on an 80-degree day. Pine needles and oak leaves pad the trail. This was particularly evident when we hiked the trail in the fall of 1993. Earlier hail storms had ripped small branches, leaves, acorns, and pine needles from the trees, thus adding to the trail cushion.

Besides the qualities of the route, this section of the Bradshaw Mountains is a refreshing place to visit in fall. By late September or early October the big-tooth maples that grow in most of the wet canyon bottoms have turned a resplendent and brilliant red. The leaves of New Mexico locust bushes have yellowed, and the aspens have begun to turn to gold.

Access and trailhead location: Map: p. 41

To reach this trailhead from downtown Prescott, first travel east on Gurley Street for 0.3 miles to Mt. Vernon Street. From there travel south on the Senator Highway (FR 52) for approximately 11 miles to the turnoff to Mt. Union (FR 261). Continue south on FR 52 for another 2.8 miles to White Well, a wooden-covered well on the west side of the roadway. From here the trailhead is just 0.7 miles farther at the junction of Crooks Canyon and Starlight Canyon. There is a vertical fiberglass trail sign (#81) just to the right of the road. Park just below this point on the access road to the Venezia mine and mill ruins.

Road condition: The Senator Highway is paved as far as Groom Creek, then dirt, but suitable for all vehicles.

Hiking time: 1 hour.   *Length:* 1.8 miles.

Difficulty: Easy.   *Use:* Light.

Uses permitted: Hiking, horseback riding, cycling (including motorized).

Recommended seasons of use: spring, summer, fall. This portion of the Senator Highway is usually closed by deep snow by midwinter.

Maps, other resources: Prescott National Forest, west half; U.S.G.S. topographic 7.5' quad for Groom Creek.

Trail description:

The first 0.2 miles of trail are steep, though the trail is easy to follow and the footing smooth. Beyond here the trail climbs more gradually along the southeast flank of Ash Creek Ridge.

At 1.4 miles the trail becomes much wider, following what appears to have been an old wagon road. The downslope side of the trail has been maintained with well-constructed rock retaining walls. This old road, however, soon turns south while our trail continues to climb to the ridge.

At mile 1.7, just before reaching Ash Creek Ridge, you will get a splendid view of Mt. Union and the high ridge to the south.

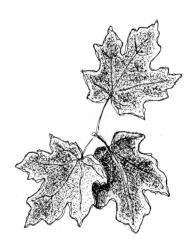

Bigtooth Maple

Finally, at mile 1.8 you will reach the Ash Creek Ridge and a good view of the valleys and mountains to the west.

At this point Trail #81 intersects both the Ash Creek Ridge road and Trail #281. Your direction from here depends only on your energy, time, and the logistics of your motorized transportation. You could travel Trail #281 (described elsewhere in this book) back to the Senator Highway, exiting just 0.3 miles south of the Mt. Union road. This distance would be about 5 miles. You can travel north on the Ash Creek Ridge road back to the Senator Highway, a distance of about 3.6 miles. You could also turn south for about 50 yards to the east leg of Trail #281 and return to the Senator Highway just north of Palace Station. This would leave you 1.4 miles south of the Trail #81 trailhead.

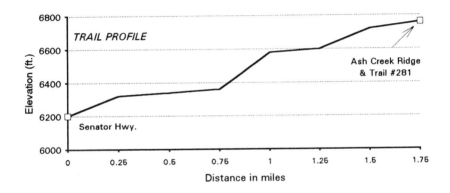

YANKEE DOODLE TRAIL #284

General information:

The Yankee Doodle Trail is over 13 miles in length. It runs from near Big Bug Mesa road south to where it ends on Senator Highway about 1 mile east of Palace Station. I will describe only the portion of the trail north of Mt. Union.

Since the trail follows a high elevation ridge, there are panoramic views in all directions. This ridge overlooks Big Bug Mesa to the east and Spruce Mountain and South Spruce Ridge to the west. Walker and the Lynx Creek drainage lie just west of and below the Mt. Union-Mt. Davis ridge.

This area offers many different recipes for hiking or riding its trails. There are round-trip opportunities that require only a single vehicle. Longer one-way trips are also possible if you use two vehicles, placing one at one end of the trail and the second at the other end.

Access and trailhead location: Map: p. 41

To reach the trailhead on Mt. Union, first go east on Gurley Street from downtown Prescott for about 1/2 mile to Mt. Vernon Street. Drive south from Prescott for approximately 11 miles to the turnoff to Mt. Union (FR 261). Turn east on FR 261 for 2 miles to the summit of Mt. Union.

To reach the north trailhead, go east on Highway 69 from downtown Prescott for 6.4 miles to the traffic light at the Walker-Lynx Lake road. Drive south for 6.8 miles to the Big Bug Mesa road (FR 670). Turn left here and follow this road for 2.7 miles to a 4-road junction. Park here. The trail can be reached by way of FR 9404K (4WD), the sign for which is at this junction.

To reach Trail #285, which is the Potato Patch access to Trail #284, travel south on the Walker Road for 10.4 miles. Turn left at the sign for Potato Patch and then stay left through this residential area. Park at the end of Poachers Row in a small parking pulloff. Then walk up the trail to a point to where you see an unmarked 4" x 4" post with a rock cairn beside it. Take the trail to the left here.

Road condition: FR 52, FR 261, and FR 670 are suitable for all vehicles if dry and free of snow.

Hiking time: 2 hours. *Length:* 3.9 miles.

Difficulty: Moderate. *Use:* Light.

Uses permitted: Hiking, horseback riding, and bicycling (non-motorized).

Recommended seasons of use: spring, summer, fall

Maps, other resources: Prescott National Forest, west half; U.S.G.S. topographic 7.5′ quad for Groom Creek.

Trail description:

I will start this description from the picnic area below the Mt. Union Fire Lookout. The south face of the sign just north of the picnic area shows destinations if you continue straight on this trail: Poland Rd. #261 (0.5 miles), Yankee Doodle Peak (2.5 miles), and Senator Hwy. (4 miles). It is directing you to the eastern extension of FR #261 and the southern extension of Trail #284. The north face of this sign directs you left (northwest): Mt. Davis Trail (0.5 miles), Pine Creek Trail #289 (0.5 miles), Potato Patch (3 miles). Go left (northwest) here.

Within a few yards the trail coming around the west flank of Mt. Union and just below the tower, merges with Trail #284. Continue to the right. The trail soon moves to the east face of the ridge through groves of small Gambel oaks. The terrain, lacking a tree overstory, provides some great views to the east of the Big Bug Mesa and the canyons draining the east side of the Bradshaw Mountains.

At 0.3 miles there is an S-shaped squeeze-through gate. Then at 0.7 miles as the trail approaches the broad saddle between Mt. Union and Mt. Davis, it merges with an old road. Here the trail passes through a cut in logs that have been placed as a barrier to vehicles. Just to the left of this barrier, however, is another wiggle-through gate that accesses a spur trail (#285) that descends steeply along the upper drainage of the Hassayampa River to Potato Patch, a distance of 1.8 miles. To continue on Trail #284, go north through the log barrier; ignore the road that goes to the right.

At 1.0 miles you must go through a wire gate. Just beyond here you will encounter a trail sign: Snowdrift Mine Rd. (0.75 miles), Big Bug Rd. (0.5 miles). Travel left.

At 1.7 miles you will pass through an area scarred by the 1972 Battle Fire. Note the blackened bark of the trunks of live trees. There are also large openings in the forest composed only of young oaks. This would suggest a fire in this area that reached and killed the crowns of trees only in patches. The southern section of Trail #284 south of Mt. Union passes through an area where the fire removed most of the pine forest.

At 2.4 miles you will reach a Trail #284 sign. Continue along the road here for another 0.3 miles to a road sign for FR 9494K (4WD). Turn sharply right and climb this very steep and rocky section of road (actually a fire-break built during the 1972 Battle Fire).

Finally, at 3.9 miles this rugged road intersects a private road marked by a "Dead-end Road" sign. Continue to the right here for another few yards to the junction with the Big Bug Mesa road.

Tip!

The Mt. Union area trails offer a number of opportunities for either one-way or round-trip hikes or rides.

Mt. Union to Big Bug Road (one-way): Park one vehicle on the north end of the trail described above. Then drive the second vehicle south on Walker Road (FR 197) to Senator Hwy. (FR 52). Drive south on this road for about 1.5 miles to the Mt. Union road (FR 261). Drive the 2 miles to the Mt. Union summit and park the second vehicle.

Potato Patch to Mt. Union to Potato Patch (round-trip): Three trails leave Potato Patch on the Hassayampa River. The rightmost trail goes almost due south, climbing steeply away from the drainage and ending in the Mt. Pine Acres residential area. There is a blazed trail from there to Mt. Union, but you probably need to inquire locally for its location.

The middle trail, which is the more direct route to Mt. Union, passes the sign for Trail #285 and follows a primitive road up the left (north) side of a creek. At mile 1.1 the trail appears to end at a mine tailings. Follow the mine road to where it intersects the Mt. Union road (about 0.5 miles). Go left on this road (FR 261A) to the summit and the trailhead for Trail #284. Go north on the trail to Mt. Davis as described above. Then, at 0.7 miles, go through the wiggle-gate to the left of the main trail. Descend to the west for 1.7 miles back to the Potato Patch area where you parked. You will have descended on the third and northern most of the three trails leaving that spot. This will comprise a round-trip of approximately 4 miles.

Another alternative is to ascend Trail #285 from Potato Patch as described above. Go through the wiggle-gate at the ridge and then proceed north past Mt. Davis to the Big Bug Mesa road. This would comprise approximately 3.5 miles. This would also require a vehicle shuttle arrangement. The profile presented below represents this route.

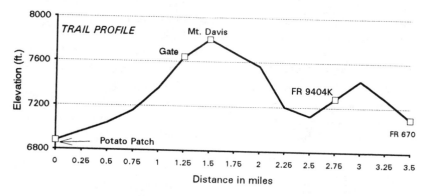

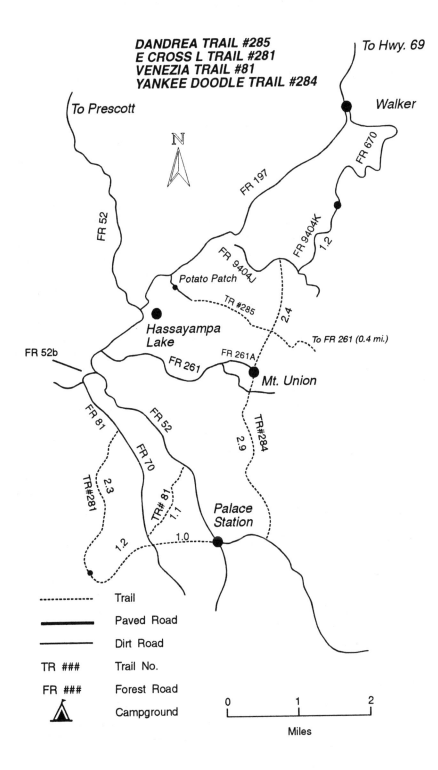

DANDREA TRAIL #285
E CROSS L TRAIL #281
VENEZIA TRAIL #81
YANKEE DOODLE TRAIL #284

To Hwy. 69

To Prescott

Walker

N

FR 670

FR 197

FR 52

FR 9404K

1.2

FR 9404J

Potato Patch

TR #285

2.4

To FR 261 (0.4 mi.)

Hassayampa
Lake

FR 261

FR 261A

FR 52b

Mt. Union

FR 81

FR 52

TR#284

2.9

TR#281

2.3

FR 70

TR# 81

1.1

Palace
Station

1.2

1.0

----------- Trail

━━━━━ Paved Road

——— Dirt Road

TR ### Trail No.

FR ### Forest Road

Campground

0   1   2

Miles

MAVERICK RIDGE TRAIL

General information:

This trail is part of a system of trails established by the Boy Scouts of America, Grand Canyon Council, in cooperation with the U.S. Forest Service. The route, following mainly forest roads, traverses the south and southwest sides of Mt. Tritle and then goes west along the ridge connecting Mt. Tritle and Maverick Mountain. Mt. Tritle, at 7,800 feet in elevation is Prescott's most visible mountain, partly because it retains a snow cover in most years well into May.

This is an exciting high elevation trail for several reasons. Since the route passes to the south side of Mt. Tritle, it avoids deep snow and is likely to be accessible longer than more northern exposure routes. Also, since the start of the trail is on a warm southerly exposure, the vegetation is mostly chaparral. Consequently, the vistas from here are unobstructed through about a 120 degree arc. Lookout Mountain can be seen to the south and Peeples Valley to the west. The route also overlooks a deep rugged canyon, a tributary of Slate Creek, leading up to Lookout Mountain.

The vegetation along this trail varies enormously. On the warm south slopes of Mt. Tritle dense chaparral dominates the landscape. As you travel the Maverick Ridge you enter a dense overstory of old trees. At this high elevation the mixed conifer type consists of large Douglas fir, white fir, and ponderosa pine.

Access and trailhead location: MapL p. 47

From East Gurley Street in Prescott turn south on the Senator Highway (Mt. Vernon St.) and go 12 miles. You will pass the turnoff to Hassayampa Lake and Walker, and the road to Mt. Union (FR 261). Just 0.3 miles past the road to Mt. Union, FR 52B turns right (west). If you lack a high-clearance vehicle, park on the main road and walk FR 52B from here.

Road condition: The access road (FR 52) is generally suitable when dry for all vehicles at least as far as this trailhead. Though rough in spots, it poses no clearance problems.

Hiking time: 3 hours

Length: 3.4 miles to the saddle just east of Maverick Mtn.

Difficulty: Moderate   *Use:* Light

Uses permitted: All uses permitted, though the road along Maverick ridge is barricaded, effectively barring anything wider than a 2-wheeled vehicle.

Recommended season of use: spring, summer, fall

Maps, other resources: Prescott National Forest, west half; U.S.G.S. topographic 7.5' quad for Groom Creek.

Trail description:

Within just a short distance along FR 52B you will come to a fork in the road. The right fork goes to a mine tailings and ends. Continue left. This portion of the trail passes through an attractive mixed conifer forest of Douglas fir, white fir, ponderosa pine, and Gambel oak. The white fir growing at high altitudes in association with pine, is a beautiful silvery barked tree having long soft upturned needles. Cones seen usually near the tree top look like upright cigars. When we last hiked this trail, there was an abundance of terminal needle bundles and cone scales on the ground, clipped by the tassel-eared (Abert) squirrel.

At mile 0.3 there is a large road sign at a road junction. The left fork is FR 81 to the Golden Eagle Mine, the right fork to Mt. Tritle and the Davis Dunkirk Mine. Stay right. Within a short distance you will come to a cattle guard and then an open vista point from where you can see the Peeples Valley area.

At 0.6 miles the country becomes more dramatic. The vegetation changes from the conifer overstory to an arid chaparral vegetation type and its typical mix of brush and small evergreen oaks. To the left of the trail a deep canyon plunges west from Lookout Mountain; to the right beside the road there are ledges of metamorphic rock, stained yellow to deep rust-red.

At 0.9 miles the trail turns right leaving FR 52B. If you look carefully to the right of this intersection, you will see an old weathered wood sign with an arrow pointing right. A small "T" in its lower right corner apparently indicates the direction to Mt. Tritle. At this point you will begin a long steep climb of over 500 feet along a very rocky road to just below the summit of Mt. Tritle.

At 1.1 miles there are mine tailings beside the road. The road to the left here ends at the mine. Continue right. Within another 0.5 miles you will pass an old ore loading chute, disintegrated, a stark weathered white.

At 1.6 miles you will reach a fork in the road. The right fork goes to the summit of Mt. Tritle, a climb of about 380 feet in 0.3 miles. The left fork

White Fir

goes west along a ridge to Maverick Mountain.

The descent from Mt. Tritle to the Maverick ridge is steep and passes through a ponderosa pine forest that includes some very old large diameter "yellow-bark" pines. White fir and groves of Gambel oak also occur here.

At 2.1 miles the trail exits the pine forest to a more open chaparral type and a grandiose view to the west of over 120 degrees. To your left on an azimuth of 160 degrees is Lookout Mountain. The road (trail) then heads for a second saddle. The descent to this saddle is extremely rocky and hikers need to be very careful of their footing. At the midway point of this rocky grade a trail goes right, skirting the worst of this loose rocky road. It then returns to the road at the saddle itself. Also at this point there is a barricade across the road, denying access to 4-wheeled vehicles.

At 3.1 miles you will reach a saddle immediately below Maverick Mountain. This is probably a good turn-around point for a day hike. There is in this vicinity another trail that was established years ago by the Boy Scouts. It leaves the Maverick Ridge and heads roughly northeast. It connects to FR 79A and Kendall Camp and other forest roads. I was unable to find this connector trail. It is a marked trail and occurs somewhere in the northeast quarter of Sec. 33, R2W T12.5N of the Groom Creek topographic quad.

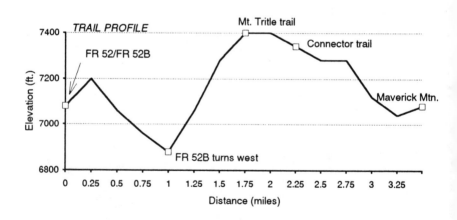

RIVER TRAIL

General information:
This trail follows forest roads to the Hassayampa River and then goes south to Kendall Camp. The trail name applied here is not an official one, but one I have used to emphasize the beautiful one-mile section of the trail that parallels the Hassayampa River.

Access and trailhead location: Map: p. 47
From East Gurley Street in Prescott, turn south on the Senator Highway (Mt. Vernon St.) and travel approximately 7 miles south through Groom Creek to where the pavement ends. Just beyond the end of the pavement turn right (west) on the road to the Summit Pine Camp (FR 97). Go due west on this road for 1.1 miles to the Lower Wolf Creek Campground on the left of the road. Our trail begins on the forest road (FR 74) that leaves the south side of the campground and crosses Wolf Creek. When the campground is closed to public use during the winter months, this road is also closed by a steel gate to vehicle access.

Road condition: FR 52 (Senator Highway) and FR 97 are suitable for all vehicles when dry and snow-free.

Hiking time: 2.5 hours.   *Length:* 3.25 miles

Difficulty: Easy   *Use:* Heavy

Uses permitted: Motorized use permitted.

Recommended season of use: Spring, summer, fall.

Maps, other resources: Prescott National Forest, west half; U.S.G.S. topographic 7.5′ quads for Groom Creek.

Trail description:
The trail leaves the south side of the Lower Wolf Creek Campground and crosses Wolf Creek. Just after crossing the creek you will encounter a gate across the road (FR 74), locked during the months when the campground is closed. Within about 0.25 miles you will pass some large granite boulders on the south side of the road. There is a grand view from these rocks of the Sierra Prietas and the northern Bradshaw Mountains. Mt. Francis can be seen on an azimuth of 302 deg., Mt. Tritle at 148 deg., and Maverick Mtn. at 225 deg. These azimuths assume that you have already set a declination constant of 14 deg. on the compass.

The road from here descends through stands of tall dense brush and evergreen oaks to the wooded drainage of the Hassayampa River.

At 0.5 miles the road forks at a large highway sign. The road west goes to Payoff Spring at the base of Maverick Mountain, a distance of 2 miles. Continue east descending gradually into a cooler pine covered forest area. At about 0.8 miles you will pass through an attractive park-like clearing, huge boulders dotting the area as if carefully placed by a landscape architect.

At 1.25 miles you will reach a crossing of the Hassayampa River marked by a large highway sign. The right (west) fork goes to Payoff Spring, a distance of 1.25 miles; our route goes east from here parallel to the river, and at this point becomes FR 79B. Be aware that during the summer and winter rainy seasons this river may have extremely high flow volumes. You can get some idea of what the river looks like in flood from the height at which high water has lodged debris in trees and rocks above the creek bed. Never attempt to cross this river during flood.

For the next half-mile or so the trail becomes a beautiful river walk. The road stays on a bench just above the river itself which in this area flows through a small granite gorge. This cool canyon has really diverse vegetation. Above the river you will see an occasional Douglas fir among the ponderosa pines, evidence of the cool moist nature of this drainage. In the river channel is a typical gallery forest of deciduous trees and shrubs.

At 1.8 miles a road turns sharply west to a dead-end at Gold Strike Mine #2 (private property). Continue east on FR 79B for about 0.6 miles to its junction with FR 79. FR 79 goes south, crossing the Hassayampa River, and continues for another 0.5 miles. At that point a sign shows that FR 79A goes to the right. Take this latter road for another 0.3 miles to Kendall Camp. The area is an old homestead, probably serving a mining camp. There are many fruit trees and building foundations to mark the early human habitation here. This area is an excellent camping or picnic site. From here you can explore farther west or climb to the Maverick ridge on the old Boy Scout trail marked by a sign at the corner of the Kendall Camp area.

A connecting trail to the Senator Highway goes east along the ridge between Maverick Mountain and Mt. Tritle. It is described in this guide as the "Maverick Ridge Trail."

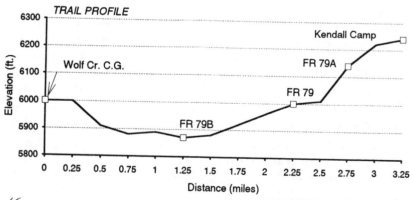

46

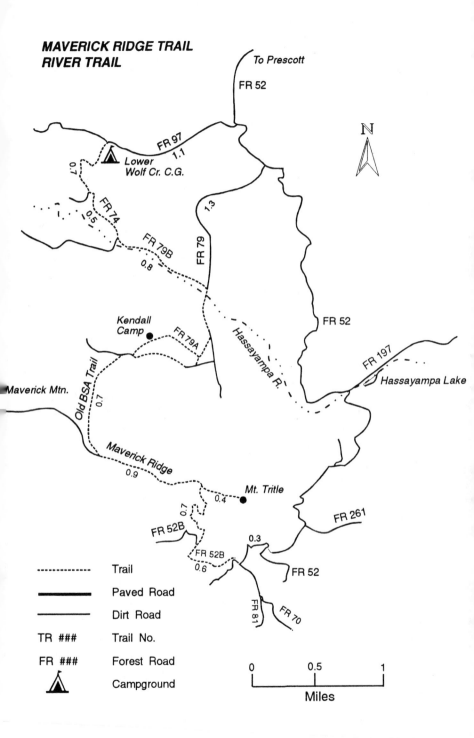

MAVERICK RIDGE TRAIL
RIVER TRAIL

To Prescott

FR 52

FR 97 1.1

Lower
Wolf Cr. C.G.

0.7

FR 74 0.5

FR 79B 0.8

FR 79

1.3

FR 52

Kendall
Camp

FR 79A

Hassayampa R.

FR 197

Hassayampa Lake

Maverick Mtn.

Old BSA Trail

0.7

Maverick Ridge

0.9

Mt. Tritle

0.4

0.7

FR 261

FR 52B

FR 52B

0.6

0.3

FR 52

FR 81

FR 70

N

- - - - - - - Trail

━━━━━━ Paved Road

──────── Dirt Road

TR ###   Trail No.

FR ###   Forest Road

△ Campground

0   0.5   1

Miles

LYNX LAKE TRAIL #311

General information:

The 55-acre Lynx Lake, about 6 miles north of Walker, at an elevation of 5,520 feet, was built in 1958 by the Arizona Game and Fish Department as a trout fishing lake. This earthen dam was actualy built on the site of an earlier dam started in 1890. This latter structure was made of concrete and was intended to serve the hydraulic placer mining operations downstream. A series of storms caused significant damage to the dam and it was never repaired. You can still see evidence of the extensive gold dredging that once occurred here in the banks of boulders and gravel that line Lynx Creek where it enters the lake.

The new dam has created a very popular area for boating, fishing, picnicing, and hiking. There is a lakeshore trail that loops completely around the lake, beginning at the lake's southern end. It is an attractive walk of about 2.5 miles that stays close to the shore for its entire length. Being close to the lake, the walk also provides a chance to observe aquatic and other birds, especially during spring and fall migrations.

Access and trailhead location:

From downtown Prescott drive east on Hwy. 69 for 4.4 miles to the traffic light at Walker Road. Turn right (south) and drive and additional 2.8 miles to the turnoff to Lynx Lake. This junction is just 0.5 miles south of the Lynx Lake Campground entrance. The parking area for the lakeshore trail is to the left of the road, just 0.4 miles from the Walker Road.

Road condition: Paved.

Hiking time: 1.5 hours   *Length:* 2.5 miles

Difficulty: Easy.   *Use:* Heavy

Uses permitted: Hiking only.

Recommended season of use: spring, summer, fall

Maps, other resources: Prescott National Forest, west half; U.S.G.S. topographic 7.5′ quads

Trail description:

We have not presented a profile of elevation and distance for this trail because the trail is quite level for its entire length. It never climbs above the lake shore for more than about 20-30 feet in elevation.

The trail leaves the parking area and goes along the west shore of the lake. For the first 0.1 miles the smooth gravel trail is about 4 feet wide and quite suitable even for wheel chairs. Beyond this point, however, the trail becomes a narrow foot path. This is quite a pleasant walk through here as the trail winds around the many small coves. Cattails and other aquatic plants fill these coves, making them attractive habitat for redwing blackbirds, leopard frogs, and brilliant red-orange dragon flies.

At 0.8 miles you will reach the trail to the marina and store. Stay to the right to continue along the lakeshore trail. At 1.0 miles you will have to cross the dam spillway in order to reach the east side of the lake. If there is water on the spillway ramp be careful; it is likely to be very slippery. Then cross to the east shore on the earthen dam.

At 1.3 miles, as the trail circles around a long cove, you will note a large ponderosa pine trimmed of most of its branches. Atop the tree is a wooden platform, intended to attract nesting ospreys. This and a few other platforms like it were constructed by the Prescott Audubon Society in cooperation with the U.S. Forest Service. To date these platforms have not been used by ospreys.

At 2.0 miles you will reach Lynx Creek. The inlet to the lake is a really attractive spot with its willow-lined creek banks and other riparian vegetation. After you cross the creek the trail is a little hard to follow where it merges with the banks of placer tailings. Look for the well used path across the top of the tailings piles.

At 2.2 miles you will reach the paved parking area. Continue along the lakeshore through the parking and boat launching area to the lakeside trail parking area just 0.2 miles farther.

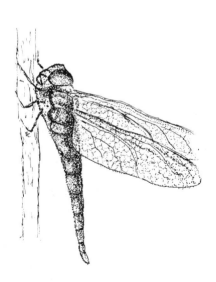

Granite Mountain

THOUGH HARDLY THE HIGHEST MOUNTAIN IN THE REGION at 7,600 feet in elevation, it nonetheless seems so in its isolation. The mountain lies at the center of Granite Mountain Wilderness, over 9,700 acres of rugged, boulder strewn landscape. Congress created the wilderness designation for this area in 1984. It is often referred to as an urban wilderness because of its proximity (only about 8 miles) to the city of Prescott.

Because of this fact and because a very popular recreation site sits at the mountain's base, citizens of this region have become vigilant. They are protective of the wilderness character of the mountain. The U.S. Forest Service has planned a very significant expansion of the campground, day-use areas, and changes to the locations of trailheads at the Granite Basin Recreation Area. Environmental groups and individuals, fearing a severe human impact from this development on the wilderness character of Granite Mountain mounted a campaign to scale back the planned improvements. Their actions and the response within the local communities appear to have caused the Forest Service to review their development alternatives.

The Granite Basin Recreation Area is 5,600 feet in elevation at the southern base of Granite Mountain. Now there are 18 campsites, 7 picnic sites, vault toilets, and a small fishing lake. The extent of the improvements will have to await more review by Forest administrators.

Though there is but a single maintained trail into the wilderness, many good trails skirt its boundaries. Many of these were once roads or trails that gave access by horse or vehicle to cattle waters and natural springs. The Forest Service has now prohibited vehicle use on some of these trails thus enhancing the quality of quieter sojourns into these wild places.

CEDAR SPRINGS TRAIL #41

General information:

This trail is another link in the system of trails serving Granite Mountain Wilderness. It is another of the recreational trails in this area that were originally roads built mostly in the late 1800's to provide horseback access to springs and other cattle waters. They were later adopted by the Prescott National Forest as part of the overall transportation system on the Forest. Many of these old unmaintained roads are now being closed or converted to recreational trails. This trail is an approach to the Granite Mountain Wilderness from the southwest. The portion of the trail beyond Red Hill Tank is the most attractive, offering scenic views of Granite Mountain. There are also some good frequently used camping sites in the vicinity of Red Hill Tank.

The trail west of Red Hill Tank is probably not too attractive to hikers. It is approximately 1.6 miles to the wilderness boundary and Trail #41 from where you must park anything other than a 4WD vehicle. It traverses relatively level terrain and there is little diversity in the vegetation. For horseback riders, though, with their ability to cover somewhat greater distances than hikers, this trail offers a chance to explore the extensive area bordering the southern boundary of Granite Mountain Wilderness. The road access to the trail is rough and rocky and not well suited to use by bicyclists.

Access and trailhead location: Map: p. 63

Drive north from downtown Prescott on Montezuma St. (becomes Whipple) to the 4-way intersection with Whipple, Miller Valley, Willow Springs, and Iron Springs Roads. Go west on Iron Springs Road for approximately 8.4 miles to the junction with Contreras Road (FR 336). Go northwest on this road for about 3.8 miles to the intersection with FR 102. Go north on FR 102 for 2.1 miles, at which point you will cross a cattle guard. FR 41 turns east just north of the cattle guard. Take FR 41 for 0.3 miles to a road junction; the left fork goes to Cowboy Tank, the right fork to Red Hill Tank. Turn right for 0.3 miles to an underpass beneath the Sante Fe railroad. Proceed through the underpass and then turn left (north).

The road beneath the Santa Fe railroad grade can become impassable when flooding of Tonto Wash deposits deep sand here, as happened during late spring of 1993.

If accessible, take FR 671 north and then east for 1.6 miles to a hinged metal gate. Just beyond the gate FR 41 continues northeast along but outside of the wilderness boundary. Trail #41, though lacking any signs to identify it, turns southeast to Red Hill Tank and Cedar Spring. Just beyond the spring it intersects Trail #39 to Blair Pass.

Road condition: Paved along Iron Springs Road, then dirt on Contreras Road (FR 336); FR 41 is suitable for high clearance vehicles; FR 671 is suitable for 4WD vehicles.

Hiking time: 1.3 hrs.

Length: 3.75 miles from wilderness boundary sign to Trail #39.

Difficulty: Moderate   *Use:* Light

Use restrictions: No motorized equipment is permitted from the Wilderness boundary to Red Hill Tank; from there to Trail #39 bicycles are also prohibited.

Recommended seasons of use: Spring, fall, winter.

Maps, other resources: Prescott National Forest map, west half; U.S.G.S. topographic 7.5' quad for Jerome Canyon and Mt. Josh.

Trail Description

The approach to Trail #41 from the Sante Fe railroad track goes through rolling hilly country, covered with scattered large ball shaped alligator junipers. The roadbed is extremely rocky and water scoured, especially where it slopes, and likely to be impassable in many places to anything but a 4WD vehicle.

Near the wilderness boundary the vegetation changes to a more scrubby appearance, dominated by chaparral species: algerita (Berberis), beargrass, large junipers, scattered pinon pines, and manzanita.

The trail from the gate at the wilderness boundary follows an old road for 2 miles as far as Red Hill Tank. The road quits there, but a trail continues for an additional 1.75 miles to where it joins TR #39. The gradient is slight, climbing less than 500 feet before the trail joins with TR #39. The trail, beyond the road, is in only fair condition and in spots may be difficult to follow past Red Hill Tank; sections may be eroded or covered with brush, particularly beyond Cedar Spring.

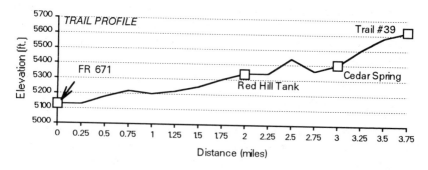

CLARK SPRING TRAIL #40

General information:

This trail is another in the network of trails serving Granite Mountain Wilderness. It provides the third leg of a loop route from Granite Mountain back to Granite Basin Lake. Hikers or riders coming south from the mountain can take Trail #37 around the west side of Little Granite Mountain. Then return to Granite Basin Lake by way of Trail #40 and Clark Spring. Trail #40 also provides campers at the Granite Basin Recreation Area with a day trip along an attractive corridor to Clark Spring.

Access and trailhead location: Map: p. 63

Drive north from downtown Prescott on Montezuma St. for 1.7 miles to the 4-way intersection. Then continue west on Iron Springs Road for approximately 3 miles to the turnoff to Granite Basin Lake (FR 374). It is then approximately 4 miles on paved road to the recreation area. As you come into the recreation site, you will approach a **STOP** sign. Continue straight. At the next road junction bear left on the dirt road (FR 374) for 0.6 miles to a wide parking area on the right. Park here and walk the 0.1 miles farther to the trailhead sign to the Clark Spring Trail (#40). The short road beyond this point will eventually be closed to vehicular traffic. A common junction for Trail #40 and Trail #261 will be established in this immediate area.

To reach the trail by way of Trail #37, drive west on Iron Springs Road from the 4-way intersection mentioned above for 6.2 miles. The trailhead sign for Trail #37 will be on the right of the highway alongside a graveled spacious parking area.

Use this access to travel Trail #40 one-way and avoid the steep ascent when traveling south from the Granite Basin Recreation area. A good plan is to use two vehicles. Park one at the northern access point described above, and the other at the trailhead for Trail #37. Hike Trail #37 south for 1.5 miles to its junction with Trail #40. Pass through the gate to the right and you will be on Trail #40. The round-trip by vehicle from the Trail #37 trailhead to the northern trailhead for Trail #40 takes only 30 minutes. It is well worth it for the one-way, downhill descent on Trail #40.

Road condition: Paved

Hiking time: 45 min.

Length: 2.0 miles; 3.5 miles if combined with Trail #37.

Difficulty: Moderate   *Use:* Moderate

Uses permitted: Hiking, horseback riding, bicycling (non-motorized)

Recommended seasons of use: Spring, fall, winter

Maps, other resources: Prescott National Forest map, west half; U.S.G.S. topographic 7.5′ quad for Iron Springs

Trail description:

This trail is in generally good condition and has a smooth surface. From Granite Basin Lake it follows a rolling course through open chaparral for about 1 mile to Clark Spring. Beyond the spring the trail begins a gradual ascent to the pass between Two Rock Mountain and Little Granite Mountain and its junction with Trail #37. This is the most attractive portion of the trail as you follow the course of a heavily scoured drainage through shady stands of ponderosa pine and Gambel oak. With water present during much of the year, the area provides habitat for a variety of wildlife species. You will most likely see tassel-eared (Aberts) squirrels, chipmunks, ground squirrels, and a variety of song birds. The wash and trail will also give evidence of the regular presence of javelina and an occasional deer. Most visible of the birds will be Stellar's jays and comical-looking acorn woodpeckers. During the cool months at least, Oregon juncos and tiny ruby-crowned kinglets will be seen flitting through the brush as you pass.

After passing Clark Spring, look on your right for a tall resinous ponderosa snag. You will find it riddled from base to top with woodpecker holes, many of them stuffed with a single acorn. This is generally the work of yearlong resident acorn woodpeckers.

The trail stays just to the east of the boundary of Granite Mountain Wilderness.

Acorn Woodpecker

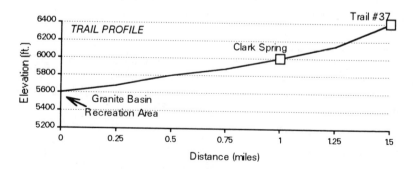

GRANITE MOUNTAIN TRAIL #261

General information:

This trail is one of the most popular on the Prescott National Forest and earns its reputation and popularity. It traverses a great variety of environs — cool streamside forest, warm brush-covered hilsides, and stark granite boulder gardens at the top of Prescott's urban wilderness. The trail lies within the Granite Mountain Wilderness, a 9,700-acre preserve that reaches to 7,600 feet in elevation. Created by Congress in 1984 as wilderness, this mountain is perhaps the most easily recognized mountain landmark within view of the city of Prescott. From its summit the views are unobstructed, partly because it is an isolated mountain island.

Access and trailhead location: Map: p. 63

You can reach this trail from the Granite Basin Recreation area. If you are coming from downtown Prescott, drive north on Montezuma St. to the 4-way intersection of Whipple, Miller Valley, Willow Springs, and Iron Springs Roads. Drive west on Iron Springs Road for approximately 3 miles to the turnoff to Granite Basin Lake (FR 374). It is then approximately 4 miles on paved road to the recreation area. As you come into the recreation site you will come to STOP sign. Continue straight. At the next road junction bear left on the dirt road (FR 374), passing the trailhead for the Clark Spring #40. You will come to a parking area and the trailhead for Trail #261. Be aware, however, that the Granite Basin Recreation Area is slated for some significant redevelopment. Current Forest Service plans call for a relocation of the trailhead away from this recreation area, the intent being to reduce recreation pressure on this wilderness trail.

Road condition: Paved to the trailhead.

Hiking time: 2.5 to 3 hours.   *Length:* 3.4 miles

Difficulty: Moderate, the climb from Blair Pass to the Granite Mountain saddle being the most difficult. The many switchbacks provide considerable relief from the steep slope.

Use: Heavy.

Uses permitted: Hiking and horseback riding only.

Recommended season of use: Spring, summer, fall, though the climb up the south facing slope of Granite Mountain could be very warm in summer.

Maps, other resources: Prescott National Forest, west half; U.S.G.S. topographic 7.5′ quads for Iron Springs and Jerome Canyon.

Trail description:

At the trailhead be sure to stop and read the information posted by the Forest Service concerning the cliff areas closed to entry during the spring. Peregrine falcons have been found nesting in the area of sheer cliffs in the southwest part of the Granite Mountain Wilderness. Populations of these birds, once widespread throughout North America, have now been greatly reduced due to certain pesticides. Research has shown that pesticide residues have moved through the food chain and ultimately affected the survival of raptor eggs by softening their shells. These birds are strong swift hunters and can dive ("stoop") at speeds up to 200 miles per hour. The peregrine is listed as a federal endangered species and occurs on Arizona's list of Threatened Wildlife Species.

Stop occasionally along the stretch of trail up to Blair Pass and use binoculars to scan the sheer cliffs of Granite Mountain. The peregrine can be recognized by the pale spots and bars of their underparts or by the streamlined appearance in flight, the wings coming to more of a point than is true of the broad-winged hawks such as the redtailed hawk. Also, the head appears to be helmeted in black.

The lower trail winds through a shaded and cool streamside lane in stands of large ponderosa pine and Emory and white oaks. When we hiked this trail in April 1993 the manzanita were already in bloom with pinkish, lantern shaped flowers.

At 0.5 miles you come in view of the sheer southwest face of Granite Mountain. When the area is not closed to protect nesting falcons, you may see climbing parties scaling these vertical cliffs.

At 0.7 miles you will see blackened tree stems, remnants of an earlier forest fire. In late spring this area is a wildflower garden. A number of herbaceous species that establish after fire occur in abundance, particularly the showy and very fragrant verbena.

At 1.3 miles you will come to the gates at Blair Pass. Just beyond the west gate is a routed-wood sign and the junction of two trails. The trail going southwest is the Little Granite Trail #37 that connects with the Clark Springs Trail #40 in 3 miles. The White Rock Trail #39 goes west from here, connecting in 2.25 miles with the Upper Pasture Trail #38. Not indicated by the sign is the fact that Trail #39 also connects with the Cedar Spring Trail #41 in just 0.8 miles. This latter trail, also described in this guide, goes northwest toward the Santa Fe railroad grade and FR 102. Our trail #261 goes through the north gate to the Granite Mountain saddle, a distance of 1 mile. The sign records that the distance to the Granite Mountain Vista is 1.25 miles. Don't believe it! This distance is much closer to 2 miles.

The trail heads almost due north from Blair Pass leaving the cool forested area for a warm south-facing brushy slope. The vegetation here is typical of much of this region — very tall silktassel, scrub oaks, mountain mahogany, pinyon pine, and alligator juniper.

These chaparral areas can be particularly attractive in spring. In early April when we hiked this trail many shrubs were blooming. Though still leafless, the squawbush, sometimes called skunk bush or lemonade berry, was in bloom. Also leafing out and blooming with its faintly greenish blossoms was the New Mexico olive. It can be recognized by its smooth bright green leaves that occur in little bundles and the little bunches of tiny green olives that eventually turn blue-black.

Although this is generally a well-maintained trail, at the time we hiked it footing was unstable because of the erosion and scouring from heavy rains of the previous winter.

Also appearing along the trail in early spring is the Indian paintbrush and the tiny purple-flowered filaree. Verbena with its rose-purple and very fragrant flower, was also abundant on the hillside.

At about 2.2 miles you will reach the saddle, marked by a wooden sign with a routed arrow pointing east, the direction to the Granite Mountain Vista. It is worth continuing straight here, taking the narrow trail north for perhaps 100 yards to some wonderful vistas to the northeast. From here on a clear day you can see the San Francisco Peaks, Kendrick Peak, Bill Williams Mountain, the redrocks of Sycamore Canyon, and the Williamson Valley area. You will not get this view from the eastern vista point. Also along this section of trail we noted the conspicuous but tiny wild candytuft, a plant with a head of densely crowded four-petaled flowers. It is a member of the mustard family.

Return to the saddle and take the trail east. This one-mile segment of trail is perhaps the most fascinating. You will first pass a giant multi-stemmed grotesquely shaped alligator juniper. Just beyond is a small grassy park that would make a fine camping spot amid the spreading branches of another massive juniper. The trail soon enters a wooded glade of big ancient yellow-bark pines — another perfect camping location. Just before reaching the overlook you will encounter another small sign that records a distance of 0.25 miles to the overlook. The trail beyond this sign is for foot traffic only. It climbs through alleys of huge granite boulders, sometimes traveling across the caprock granite itself. A few stunted aspen growing in granite fissures give testimony to the severity of weather at this site. Giant gray boulders surround the little basin just to the north of the vista point. Some are bigger than houses, their surfaces painted as if by a Bunyanesque artist in various hues of yellow to dark gray.

The various species of lichens covering these rocks produce the colors. Lichens are produced by the symbiotic or cooperative living arrangement between fungi and algae. The fungi can decompose rock and thus provide mineral nutrients to the algae, but they also envelope and feed on the photosynthetic algae. The algae do their part by supplying the fungi with organic nutrients through photosynthesis.

This area is an old-growth pine forest of large diameter ponderosa pine and a scattering of massive pine snags. These provide habitat for the rich variety of cavity-nesting birds of the region.

After traveling a total of about 3 miles, you will reach the vista point that overlooks the Granite Basin Lake area. From this point you gain a broad view of the northern Bradshaw Mountains, and the Sierra Prietas. If you do not know the various landmarks, here are some compass azimuths to identify major features: Willow Lake - 108 deg., Granite Basin Lake - 140 deg., Mt. Tritle - 155 deg., Maverick Mtn. - 160 deg., Mt. Union - 144 deg., Thumb Butte - 158 deg., and Sugarloaf Mtn. - 190 deg. These azimuths will only be correct if you have already set a declination constant of 14 deg. on your compass.

There are no alternate routes back to the Granite Basin area, so return the way you came.

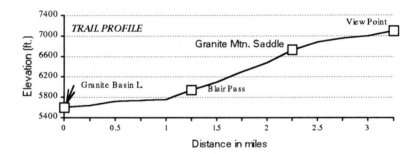

LITTLE GRANITE TRAIL #37

General information:

This trail's primary function is recreation; it is another in the network of trails providing hiking and riding recreation in and around Granite Mountain Wilderness. The trail travels along but outside the southwestern border of the wilderness, offering views of farm and ranch lands of Skull Valley. From the southern portion of the trail where it leaves Iron Springs Road, there are superb 180 degree panoramas of the Prescott area, Sugarloaf Mountain, and the western end of the Sierra Prietas. On the west side of Little Granite Mountain is evidence of the Doce Fire (1990) that burned over 300 acres of brush and woodland in this area. The area burned by this large man-caused fire has since been reseeded to stabilize the gravelly soils and restore forage for wildlife.

Access and trailhead location: Map: p. 63

To reach this trail from downtown Prescott, drive north on Montezuma St. to the 4-way intersection of Whipple, Miller Valley, Willow Springs, and Iron Springs Roads. Continue west on Iron Springs Road, for 6.2 miles to the trailhead sign. This turnoff is 3.2 miles west of the turnoff to Granite Basin Lake (FR 374). There is a graveled pull-off parking area suitable for at least 6 vehicles.

Road condition: Iron Springs Road is paved.

Hiking time: 1.5 hours   *Length:* 3.3 miles

Difficulty: Moderate   *Use:* Light

Uses permitted: Hiking, horseback riding, bicycling (non-motorized)

Recommended seasons of use: Spring, fall, winter.

Maps, other resources: Prescott National Forest map, west half; U.S.G.S. topographic 7.5' quad for Iron Springs and Jerome Canyon.

Trail description:

For the first 1.5 miles the trail travels almost due north through dense chaparral and large pinon pines and junipers. Just before the trail passes under a power line, there is a splendid view to the south of the Sierra Prietas and the Prescott area. After crossing under the power line, you will encounter a service road. The trail, however, continues on the opposite side of this road. At mile 1.5 you will reach a junction with Clark Spring Trail #40. From here you can take Trail #40 to Granite Basin Lake or continue northwest on Trail #37. The latter trail goes for another 1.2 miles around the west edge of Little Granite Mountain to meet Trail #38 where it comes in from the west.

This portion of the trail is perhaps the most enjoyable. It passes through the heart of the area burned during the Doce fire, and, contrary to what you might expect, is attractive because of that fire. Grasses seeded to stabilize the exposed soils have matured, and chaparral has grown to about 3 feet in height. The more open landscape has exposed the dramatice arrangement of boulders on this hillside and given an unobstructed view of the valleys and mountains to the west and Granite Mountain to the north.

Beyond its junction with Trail #38, Trail #37 continues for another 1.2 miles to Blair Pass and the junction with Trail #261 (wilderness area boundary) and Trail #39.

Hikers or riders coming down the Granite Mountain Trail (Trail #261) might consider using Trail #37 as an alternate return route to Granite Basin Lake. Take Trail #37 south around Little Granite Mountain to Trail #40. Then return in a gradual descent to the campground area by way of Trail #40.

If you plan a roundtrip starting and ending at the Iron Springs trailhead and parking area, I would suggest descending on Trail #37, going east on Trail #261, and then south on Trail #40. The ascent on Trail #37 from its junction with Trail #38 is quite steep, climbing almost 700 feet in elevation in just over a mile. The alternate ascent south on Trail #40 is somewhat more gradual over a greater distance.

Precautions: As with most central Arizona trails, this one has no water available. Be sure to carry sufficient water. There is untested water at Clark Spring, should you use this as a return route.

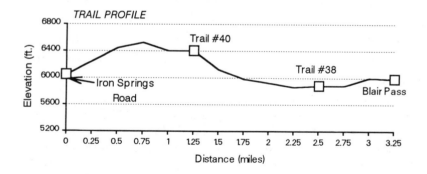

UPPER PASTURE TRAIL #38
WHITE ROCK SPRING TRAIL #39

General information:

These two short trails provide access to Granite Mountain Wilderness. Many recreational trails in this area were originally roads that were built mostly in the late 1800's to provide horseback access to springs and other cattle waters. They were later adopted by the Prescott National Forest as part of the overall transportation system. Many of these old, unmaintained roads have been closed to motor vehicles and converted to recreational trails.

The vegetation is primarily dense chaparral, pinon pine, and juniper. Tracks of coyote, bobcat, deer, and javelina were evident in the soft mud of the trail when I last traveled it.

Access to trailhead location: Map: p. 63

From downtown Prescott first drive north on Montezuma St. (becomes Whipple) to the 4-way intersection of Whipple, Willow Creek, Miller Valley, and Iron Springs Roads. Then drive west on Iron Springs Road for approximately 8.4 miles to the junction with Contreras Road (FR 336). Turn north here and drive 0.8 miles to where this dirt road passes under a power line. At this point a secondary dirt road leaves Contreras Road and goes northeast paralleling a fence. Either walk or drive this road staying to the left along the fenceline for 0.7 miles, passing a squeaky windmill and an old wooden corral (Division Well) on the left. One could probably trailer horses this far if the road is not muddy or snow covered.

Road condition: Paved on Iron Springs, then dirt on Contreras Rd.

Hiking time: Will depend on how far you take a vehicle.

Length: 2.8 miles from Contreras Road to junction of Trail #38 and Trail #37, 3.1 miles to junction with Trail #41 (via Trail #39).

Difficulty: Easy to follow trail in gently rolling terrain.

Use: Light

Uses permitted: There are no restrictions on the road approaches to this trail, but no motorized equipment is permitted on Trail #38 east beyond mile 1.8 at the barricade.

Recommended seasons of use: Spring, fall, winter

Maps, other resources: Prescott National Forest map, west half; U.S.G.S. topographic 7.5′ quad for Iron Springs

Trail description:

The road approach to Trail #38 after it leaves Contreras Road travels northeast along a fenceline. At mile 0.7 you will pass an old squeaky windmill and wooden corrals on your left. This is Division Well. At mile 0.85, stay to the right. At mile 1.2, there is a panoramic view of the southwest side of Granite Mountain. The roadway here appears to have served as a firebreak during the 1990 Doce Fire. South of the roadway, notice the charred sticks of tall oak brush that is vigorously sprouting from its root crowns. North of the roadway, however, the chaparral is dense and mature. There is an important junction at mile 1.8 . The site is marked by a metal water trough and a log barricade. The trail signs that were here in early 1993 are now gone, presumeably vandalized. The trail to the right, past the barricade, goes to Trail #37 (Little Granite Trail), a distance of 1.2 miles. The trail to the north goes to Cedar Spring and Red Hill Tank. This trail, although not named or numbered, appears on the Prescott National Forest recreation map as Trail #39.

If you choose the northerly route, within about 0.2 miles you will come to a small pond (White Rock Spring); stay along the left bank of the pond. After traveling 0.6 miles from the trail junction the trail will cross a narrow wash. There is a worthwhile diversion here. Mark where you leave the trail and walk down this wash for 0.1 miles to a massive alligator juniper on the right of the wash. My measurement of its basal circumference was just under 29 feet. After you return to the trail, continue north for another 0.5 miles to a trail junction. The signs at the trail junction show directions west to Cedar Spring (says 0.25 miles; actually closer to 0.5 miles) and Red Hill Tank (1 mile), and east to Blair Pass (1.25 miles). The trails in both directions parallel the boundary of Granite Mountain Wilderness. Cedar Spring is a pleasant spot with small cottonwoods, willows, and evergreen oaks shading this tiny wetland.

Please note that the trail profile shown below begins at the junction of Trail #37 and Trail #38, goes *west* on Trail #38, then continues *north*.

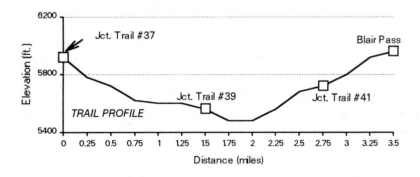

62   *GRANITE MOUNTAIN*

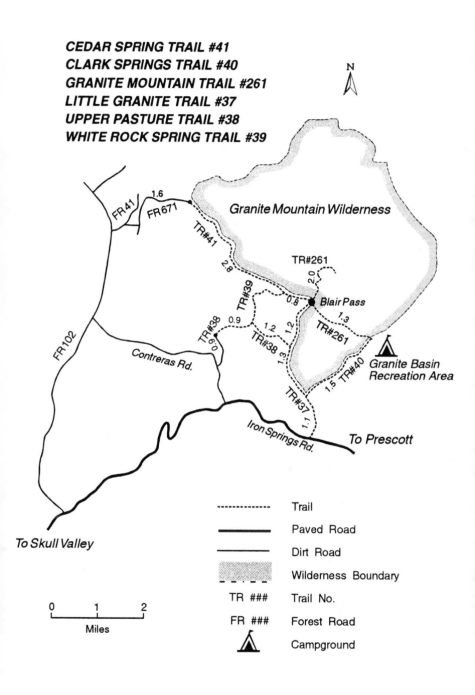

CEDAR SPRING TRAIL #41
CLARK SPRINGS TRAIL #40
GRANITE MOUNTAIN TRAIL #261
LITTLE GRANITE TRAIL #37
UPPER PASTURE TRAIL #38
WHITE ROCK SPRING TRAIL #39

N

FR41
FR671 1.6
TR#41 2.8

Granite Mountain Wilderness

TR#261
2.0

TR#39 0.8
Blair Pass

TR#38 0.9 TR#261 1.3

FR102
1.2 1.2
TR#38 .3
TR#37 .3

1.5 TR#40

Granite Basin
Recreation Area

Contreras Rd.

TR#37 1.1

Iron Springs Rd. To Prescott

To Skull Valley

----------- Trail

———— Paved Road

——— Dirt Road

░░░░░░░ Wilderness Boundary

- - - - -

TR ### Trail No.

FR ### Forest Road

△ Campground

0   1   2
Miles

MINT WASH TRAIL #345

General Description:

At present there are no signs on this trail to show distances or even a trail number. However, the trail has been recently maintained and appears on Forest Service records with the above number. This seems to suggest that it is due for some further development.

This is another in the system of trails adjacent to and within the Granite Mountain Wilderness. The trail starts at Granite Basin Lake and stays along Mint Wash for its entire length traveling just east of the Granite Mountain Wilderness. Mint Wash, although having a live stream for a good part of the year, is not scenic. The trip along this corridor, though, is worthwhile, to see an object lesson in misuse and mismanagement of what could be a beautiful and functioning riparian corridor. The deeply cut stream is almost devoid of vegetation. Each successive heavy runoff of either snow-melt or rainfall, with nothing to slow it or filter debris and silt, further deepens the channel. All of this is the result of decades of overuse by livestock.

Access to trailhead location: Map: p. 68

Road access to this trail is from the Granite Basin Recreation area. From downtown Prescott drive north on Montezuma St. (becomes Whipple) to the 4-way intersection of Iron Springs, Miller Valley, Willow Creek, and Whipple roads. Drive west on Iron Springs Rd. for approximately 3 miles to the turnoff to Granite Basin Lake (FR 374). It is then 3.6 miles on paved road to the recreation area. As you come into the recreation site you will reach a STOP sign. Turn right at the STOP and within a short distance you will see a "Day use only" sign. Turn right again, crossing the concrete ramp and ending at the parking lot next to the spillway for Granite Basin Lake.

Road condition: Paved on Iron Springs Road and on the road to the Granite Basin Recreation area.

Hiking Time: 1.5 hours   *Length:* 3 miles

Difficulty: Easy   *Use:* Light

Uses permitted: Hiking, horseback riding, bicycles (non-motorized)

Recommended seasons of use: Spring, fall, winter

Maps, other resources: Prescott National Forest map, west half; U.S.G.S. topographic 7.5′ quad for Iron Springs and Jerome Canyon.

Trail description:

From the parking area near the lake spillway, walk north past the right side of the spillway descending to the creek. Cross the creek about

50 yards below the spillway to the trail that travels along the west side of Mint Wash. Ponderosa pines mixed with junipers and pinyon pines dominate the vegetation within this steep walled canyon. The stream channel here is particularly ugly, deeply cut and scoured by successive heavy runoff events. At 0.2 miles you will pass through a hinged gate.

At 0.5 miles, if you look across the creek, you will see eroded stream banks as much as 10 feet in height. The roots of mature trees perch perilously at the edge, the roots snaking into midair. As the canyon begins to widen, you will see a distinct difference in vegetation between the east and west sides of the canyon. The trail being on the warmer west side passes mostly through semi-arid vegetation such as pinon pines, juniper, and chaparral species. Tall dead stalks of century plants dot the hillside below the rocky granite bluffs of Granite Mountain. You will soon come into an attractive little grove of deciduous trees within the flood zone but above the actual channel — mostly ashes, and walnuts. The presence of these species indicates that the water table here remains high enough to support these riparian trees and that the stream channel itself would likely support the establishment of riparian vegetation were it given the chance. However, there was absolutely no understory of seedling or sapling trees in this area.

At 1.1 miles the trail crosses to the east side of the creek and within another 0.1 miles crosses back again to the west side. Deer, coyote, and bobcat tracks were evident here.

At mile 1.8, the trail becomes difficult to follow. The stream is broad with great piles of debris deposited during past floods. You will need to pick your way through this area as best you can, eventually rejoining the trail below this debris choked area.

At 3.1 miles you will come to a wire gate across a 4-wheel drive road on the east side of Mint Wash. The trail apparently ends here at its junction with Trail #347 (fiberglass sign here indicates Trail #47) and FR 9261Y. This road goes east and then north for 1.7 miles to the Central Yavapai Fire District, Station #2 at Williamson Valley Road.

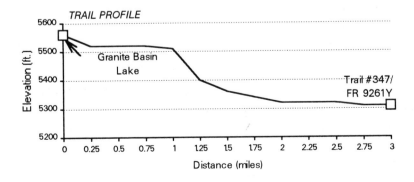

GRANITE MOUNTAIN

WILLOW TRAIL #347

General information:

January 2, 1993, was a less than perfect day on which to hike and document this trail. The temperature was in the mid 40's, a strong wind was blowing, and thickening clouds signaled the approach of a Pacific storm. The ground was saturated from recent rains, and mud quickly balled on cleated boots. I would not recommend this trail after heavy rains have softened the trail surface.

The trailhead sign shows that the trail number is #47, although this has been redesignated #347 on current Forest Service maps.

This trail has few outstanding features to attract hikers. It does, however, offer both hikers and horseback riders a short, pleasant, easy route to the Granite Basin Recreation area from the Ho Kay Gan residential area in Prescott. It also gives equestrians some extensive areas for riding when this trail is combined with connecting 4-wheel drive roads. The trail extends for about 5 miles to Mint Spring at the edge of the Granite Mountain Wilderness. From there it connects with FR 9261Y that goes north to the Central Yavapai Fire Station.

Access to trailhead location: Map: p. 68

To reach the eastern end of this trail, drive north on Montezuma St. (becomes Whipple) from downtown Prescott. Continue to the 4-way intersection of Whipple, Miller Valley, Willow Springs, and Iron Springs Roads. Take Iron Springs Road west for 1.2 miles to Williamson Valley Road. Take this road north for 1.3 miles to where the road crosses Willow Creek. Just 0.1 miles farther turn left on Burnt Ranch Rd., then an immediate right onto Hozoni Rd. and travel for 0.1 miles. Turn left onto Katahn Dr. and continue west for about 0.4 miles to Yeibitchi Dr. At this junction there is a "Dead End" sign on the road to the left. Continue in this direction to the large green steel gate. There is a vehicle parking area next to the gate. The trailhead is marked by a vertical fiberglass post located on the north side of this parking area.

Road condition: Paved.

Hiking time: 1.5 hours to FR 374.   *Length:* 2.3 miles to FR 374.

Difficulty: Easy   *Use:* Light

Uses premitted: Hiking, horseback riding, bicycling (non-motorized)

Recommended seasons of use: Spring, fall, winter

Maps, other resources: Prescott National Forest map, west half; U.S.G.S. topographic 7.5' quads for Prescott, Iron Springs, and Jerome Canyon.

Trail description:

The trail starts just 0.5 miles east of the Willow Administrative Site at the edge of the Ho Kay Gan residential subdivision. The trail heads north for a short distance paralleling a cattle fence and then turns northwest. At 0.1 miles the trail forks, the main trail going left up the wash. The trail then goes almost due west staying alongside a barbed-wire fence. The trail passes through stands of mature chaparral consisting of mountain mahogany, scrub oak, cliffrose, and other chaparral species. Mule deer feed heavily on cliffrose especially during early summer drouth when succulent annuals may not be available. Other wildlife, other than song birds, likely to be seen in this area, include javelina, owls, hawks, and an occasional rattlesnake. In warm seasons, watch where you step, especially in the washes.

At 0.5 miles you will encounter a steel horse gate. Just before reaching the gate the buildings of a U.S. Forest Service administrative site will be seen on your left. At 0.8 miles you will pass a wire gate on your left; this is an access gate to the Forest Service administrative site.

At mile 1.5 the trail passes beneath a powerline. Just beyond this point you will reach the maintenance road for this line; stay to the left along this road. Within just a few feet you will come to a triangular intersection of 4-wheel drive roads. Stay to the right here to the saddle and an iron gate. Here you will have a magnificent and unobstructed view of the east face of Granite Mountain. If you continue along this 4-wheel drive road for another 0.7 miles, you will reach the paved road (FR 374) to the Granite Mountain Recreation Area. Trail #347, however, heads northwest just after you pass through the aforementioned iron gate. It goes along an old retired road, blocked now to vehicle access by dirt banks. The trail ends at mile 5.2 at the wilderness boundary near Mint Spring. A 4-wheel drive road (FR 9261Y) heads north from here for about 1.5 miles to Williamson Valley Road.

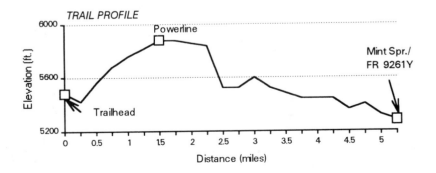

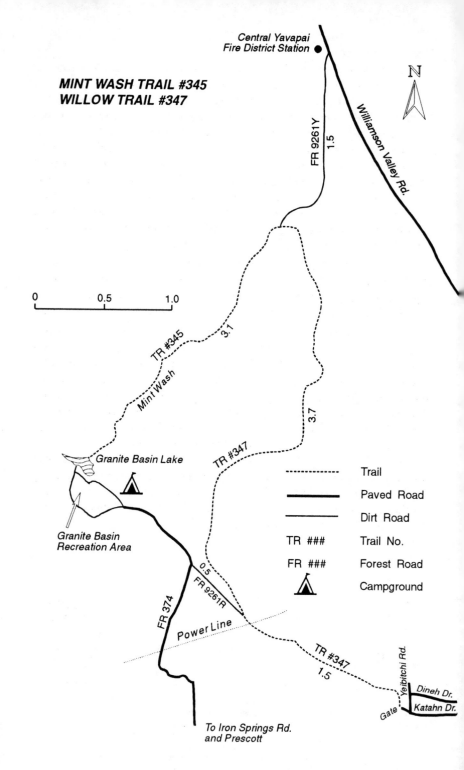

MINT WASH TRAIL #345
WILLOW TRAIL #347

Central Yavapai
Fire District Station

FR 9261Y

1.5

Williamson Valley Rd.

N

0   0.5   1.0

TR #345

3.1

Mint Wash

3.7

TR #347

Granite Basin Lake

Granite Basin
Recreation Area

FR 9261R

0.5

FR 374

Power Line

TR #347

1.5

Yeibitchi Rd.

Dineh Dr.

Gate

Katahn Dr.

To Iron Springs Rd.
and Prescott

---- Trail

—— Paved Road

— Dirt Road

TR ### Trail No.

FR ### Forest Road

⛺ Campground

Juniper Mesa

THIS 7,000 FOOT HIGH FLAT-TOPPED MESA was established by Congress in 1984 as the Juniper Mesa Wilderness. Its south-facing rim is the most spectacular topographic feature of an area that lies roughly halfway between Prescott and Seligman. The mesa is actually a portion of the Juniper Mountains, so-named many years ago by local inhabitants for the abundance of juniper trees on its slopes. Actually, there is a diverse vegetation of ponderosa pine, Utah juniper, and pinyon pine that is home to black bears, mountain lions, mule deer, wild turkey, and Aberts squirrels, to name a few of the larger wildlife species.

If you hike Trail #20 along the mesa rim, its broken rock surface will soon make you aware of the geologic origin of this mountain. This is limestone deposited during the mid-Paleozoic era. Underlying these sedimentary layers are granites and other intrusive rocks, more apparent on the lower elevation trails to the south of the rim.

This spectacular mesa has also played witness to critical events in the development of territorial Arizona. Lt. A. W. Whipple explored the Walnut creek area, which lies just below the escarpment to the south, in late 1853. He was trying to establish a suitable route for a railline from Arkansas to the Pacific. The trailhead for Trail #3 is very near the 6,000 foot pass that Whipple refers to in his journals as Aztec Pass. Nothing developed immediately from Whipple's exploration of this region. The surveys that he conducted did, however, influence later expeditions including two surveys by Lt. Edward F. Beale from 1857 to 1859. Beale was attempting to find a wagon route from Ft. Smith, Arkansas to the Colorado River (see information for Trail #3).

JUNIPER MESA TRAIL #20

General information:

Lying entirely within Juniper Mesa Wilderness, this trail offers magnificent views to the south from the mesa rim. Immediately below the rim lie the verdant valley and ranches of Walnut Creek. The irrigated pastures of the ranches scattered along this perennial stream offer a striking contrast to the rugged mountain terrain to the south. From the eastern rim one can see a vast panorama of northern Arizona — the Mogollon Rim, the major volcanic peaks from Bill Williams Mtn. to the San Francisco Peaks, and the colorful cliffs of the Sycamore Canyon Wilderness.

The Walnut Creek area also has great historical significance. It was part of a major supply route between Prescott and the Colorado River during the late 1800s. For more on this see the description of Trail #3.

The Juniper Mesa trail is relatively level at an elevation of about 7,000 ft., traversing along the mesa's rim through ponderosa pine, Gambel oak, and alligator juniper. In one of the most remote sections of northwestern Arizona, it offers the wilderness traveler an experience of solitude and vast panoramas of this semi-arid region.

Access and trailhead location: Map: p. 78

The east trailhead is at Juniper Spring at the intersection of FR 9867A and Trail #2. The approach on foot is by way of Juniper Springs Trail #2 starting from its trailhead on FR 95. To reach the trailhead for Trail #2 from Prescott, take the Williamson Valley Road north from Prescott. Stay on this road for 36 miles to the junction with FR 95. Drive west on FR 95 for about 1.5 miles to the common trailheads for Juniper Springs Trail #2 and Old Military Trail #1, just east of Walnut Creek Work Center. See the description for Trail #2 for a more thorough account of that route.

If you wish to travel by 4WD vehicle to the east trailhead, continue on FR 6 for about 15 miles, turning north at the junction with FR 95 instead of going straight to Walnut Creek. You will finally reach a junction with FR 9867A. If you reach the junction with FR 7, you have gone about 1.5 miles past the FR 9867A turnoff. Take FR 9867A southwest for about 5.5 miles to Juniper Spring. FR 9867A, however, is suitable for four-wheel drive vehicle only; the climb to the spring is steep and rough.

The west access is on top of Juniper Mesa where Trail #20 intersects Trail #3. If you plan to hike or ride Juniper Mesa Trail as part of a complete loop that incorporates Trail #3 and Trail #2, we would recommend that you travel from west to east. The approach to the mesa rim via Trail #3, while steep in places, stays in a more forested and cooler habitat than does Trail #2. See the description for Trail #3. Keep in mind also that the total distance on these three trails is about 12.5 miles.

Road condition: Except for FR 9867A, the dirt roads described are suitable for all vehicles when these roads are dry.

Hiking time: 3.5 hours   ***Length:*** 6.5 miles

Difficulty: Although this route is relatively level, I have classed it as difficult because of its length and the difficulty of the trails that provide access to it.

Use: Light

Uses permitted: Hiking and horseback riding only.

Recommended season of use: spring, summer, fall

Maps, other resources: Prescott National Forest, west half; U.S.G.S. topographic 7.5′ quads for Juniper Mountain and Indian Peak.

Trail description:

I will describe this trail from west to east beginning at the second of two wire gates on Oaks and Willows Trail #3. At this gate the trail straight ahead (south) is Juniper Mesa Trail #20, although it is not named. The trail to the left (northeast) is the continuation of the Oaks and Willows Trail #3 to Pine Spring and FR 7. Someone has scratched over the existing sign and scratched in arrows reversing the directions. These attempts to mislead travelers are incorrect. This is a dangerous bit of vandalism because this big remote country is not a place in which to get lost or confused on directions.

Mountain Lion

From this point Trail #20 passes through dense stands of old-growth pinyon pines along a limestone shelf. The trail surface is mainly loose limestone rock and footing is difficult in places. After passing through the fence the trail heads for the mesa rim and then turns east paralleling the rim. Along this stretch of trail there are wonderful views of the mountains to the south — the Santa Maria Mountains, Camp Wood Mtn., and Hyde Mtn. The latter peak can be recognized by its fire lookout.

This lookout, rather than sitting atop a steel frame, is actually a 12-foot by 12-foot wooden house, the only fire tower of this style on the Prescott National Forest. Consequently, it looks more like a little bump atop this mountain.

There were lots of scattered wildflowers along this rim trail during the spring of 1993. One of the most spectacular was the Fendler Bush, sometimes called false mockorange, a tall shrub that in places was covered with a mass of 1-inch wide white flowers. The flowers remind me of the blossoms of the eastern dogwood. It has four petals and 8 stamens, the petals being widely separated when fully open. Other flowers of note include the very common western wallflower. A member of the mustard family, it has a dense head of 4-petaled bright yellow flowers on a tall stem (2 ft.). The nearly linear leaves attach directly to the stem.

At about mile 3.1 you will come to a cattle gate. Once through it you will note that you no longer have to cross a barbed wire fence to reach the edge of the rim.

When you reach about mile 5 at the eastern side of the rim, the trail begins to take a more northeasterly direction. After crossing a level open stretch of the mesa, the trail then descends sharply through a series of switchbacks to Juniper Spring. Within about 100 yards of the spring itself you will come to the junction with Juniper Spring Trail #2 that turns sharply south. The trail sign there indicates that the mileage to FR 95 is 3.5 miles.

There is generally water at Juniper Spring, but do not depend on it. If you do use this water, be sure to treat it.

See the description of Juniper Spring Trail #2 for more information on that leg of this loop route.

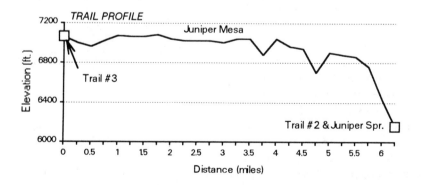

TRAIL PROFILE

72

JUNIPER SPRING TRAIL #2

General information:
This trail offers the traveler some unique and interesting views of northern Arizona. It also connects with the east end of Juniper Mesa Trail #20 which travels west across the entire Juniper Mesa Wilderness, thus offering a varied wilderness experience in one of the most remote sections of northwestern Arizona.

Access and trailhead location: Map: p. 78
Drive north on Montezuma St. to the 4-way intersection of Whipple, Miller Valley, Willow Springs, and Iron Springs Roads. Continue west on Iron Springs Rd. to Williamson Valley Road., a total distance from downtown Prescott of 3 miles. Turn north (right) and stay on this road (FR 6) for 36 miles to the junction with FR 95. Proceed west on FR 95 for about 1.5 miles. The south trailhead lies at an elevation of 5,200 ft. and starts at FR 95 just 0.2 miles east of Walnut Creek Station. The Old Military Trail #1 and the Juniper Springs Trail #2 share a common trailhead.

The north trailhead is at Juniper Spring and can be reached by way of FR 9867A. This is a four wheel drive road only, very rough, and particularly steep near Juniper Spring.

Road condition: The access road to the south trailhead on FR 95 is suitable for all vehicles.

Hiking time: 2 hours   *Length:* 3.5 miles

Difficulty: Difficult   *Use:* Light

Uses permitted: Hiking and horseback riding only.

Recommended season of use: spring, summer, fall

Maps, other resources: Prescott National Forest, west half; U.S.G.S. topographic 7.5' quad for Indian Peak.

Trail description:
As you leave the common trailheads for Trail #1 and Trail #2, follow the old road, well marked by rock cairns. At 0.1 miles you will note that there is a considerable amount of brush stacked across this road. The trail turns right here and is well marked by cairns. Continue to follow the route marked by lines of broken brush and rock cairns.

At 0.2 miles you will come to a trail sign indicating the direction and mileage to Juniper Spring. At this point you will also see brush stacked across the road to the right. The road to the right goes to an old cemetery on private land. This site is apparently a burial ground for settlers that occupied this area in the late 1800s. There is a small grave site surrounded by a decorative iron fence.

To continue on the trail, however, follow the cairn marked route. At 0.3 miles you will come to a wire gate, the boundary of the Forest Service Administrative Site. Once you cross through this gate the trail goes to the right. Just beyond the gate is another small routed wood sign indicating the direction east to the Old Military Trail #1. Its route is also marked by rock cairns. This route to the Old Military Trail was established somewhat recently as a connector to the actual roadway. Motorized travel is permitted on this route provided the vehicle does not exceed 40 inches in width (thus excluding jeeps, etc.).

At the junction with Trail #1, the Juniper Spring Trail goes almost due north climbing almost 1,000 feet in 3.5 miles to Juniper Spring. The trail is a winding one with a fairly gradual ascent to the spring. Since it goes through semi-desert country, one should be constantly aware of the possible presence of rattlesnakes either on or adjacent to the trial.

Juniper Spring is likely to have water, but of unknown quality. If you use it, be sure to treat it first.

The junction with the Juniper Mesa Trail #20 is just a few yards west of the spring.

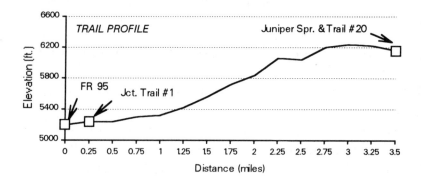

OAKS AND WILLOWS TRAIL #3

General information:

From the south trailhead this trail travels through the heavily wooded George Wood Canyon, and provides a gateway to Juniper Mesa Wilderness. Congress created this 7,640-acre wilderness in 1984 and named it for the flat-topped mesa that overlooks the Walnut Creek area from the north. By connecting with other wilderness area trails, the traveler has several options for exploring this remote part of northern Arizona.

The area is also worth exploring because of its significance to the development of territorial Arizona. Forest Road 150 along Walnut Creek lies along the route once known as Mojave Road. This was the major supply and mail road during the 1860s connecting Prescott to the ferry at Hardyville on the Colorado River, and ultimately the southern California port of San Pedro. This section of road was part of a toll road owned by Capt. William H. Hardy. The road was gated at a site just east of the current Walnut Creek Work Station (U.S. Forest Service), thus enabling the owner to collect tolls from travelers. The site was then named Toll Gate. In the spring of 1869 a military camp was established on the site and in October of the following year the name was changed to Camp Hualpai. With the threat of Indian raids having abated, this post was abandoned in July 1873.

Lt. A. W. Whipple first explored Walnut Creek in 1853 during his attempts to find and survey a path for a railroad from Arkansas to the Pacific. The trailhead for Trail #3 is very near the 6,000-foot pass that Whipple in his journals named Aztec Pass.

Today much of the bottomland along Walnut Creek remains in private ownership as a series of cattle ranches. The perennial flow of the creek with some groundwater pumping supports extensive areas of irrigated pasture. The view from the rim of Juniper Mesa provides a striking contrast in landscapes between this pastoral setting and the remote and rugged mountains to the south and west.

This wild country is home to mule deer, its chief predator the mountain lion, wild turkeys, black bear, and javelina. Besides the numerous avian species, the tassel-eared squirrels are probably the most frequently seen wildlife along the pine-covered rim.

Access and trailhead location: Map: p. 78

Drive north on Montezuma St. to the 4-way intersection of Whipple, Miller Valley, Willow Springs, and Iron Springs Roads. Continue west on Iron Springs Rd. to Williamson Valley Road., a total distance from downtown Prescott of 3 miles. Turn north (right) and stay on this road (FR 6) for 36 miles to the junction with FR 95. Just before reaching this junction, you will cross Walnut Creek on a steel bridge. Turn west on FR 95 for about 1.5 miles to the Walnut Creek Station. Just about 0.25 miles before reaching the Work Station you will pass on the right the parking area and trailheads for Trails #1 & #2. Just a few yards past the Work Station FR 95 turns south. Continue west on FR 150 passing through the gateway to the Box L Ranch. Continue west on FR 150 for about 6 miles to the trail sign on the right of the road. Just beyond the trail sign there is a nice parking and camping area to the right of the road. If you happen to pass this area you will soon come to a "Locked Gate Ahead" sign. Turn around here. FR 150 dead-ends at this locked gate, the entrance to the Luis Maria Baca Float and the O R O Ranch, and it is difficult to turn around here.

To reach the north trailhead at Pine Spring, take FR 150 east from the Walnut Creek Station for 2 miles to FR 6. Take FR 6 north for 7 miles to FR 7; take FR 7 southwest for 6 miles to the Pine Springs trailhead at the end of the road.

Road condition: From the Camp Wood turnoff the road (FR 6) is dirt, but suitable for all vehicles when dry. Likewise, FR 6 and FR 7 east and north of the Walnut Creek Work Station are also suitable for all vehicles.

Hiking time: 3 hours   *Length:* 4.9 miles

Difficulty: Moderate   *Use:* Light

Uses permitted: This trail enters the Juniper Mesa Wilderness and only hiking and horseback riding area permitted.

Recommended season of use: Spring, summer, fall.

Maps, other resources: Prescott National Forest, west half; U.S.G.S. topographic 7.5' quads for Juniper Mountain and Indian Peak.

Trail description:

The lower end of this trail follows along the east side of George Wood Canyon but above the canyon itself. It passes through rather open country of scattered ponderosa pine, evergreen oaks, and alligator junipers. For a short distance it follows an old road marked with rock cairns.

At mile 0.3 the trail climbs steeply through a series of switchbacks. The trail here is well maintained with frequent erosion control logs placed across the trail. The trail soon enters an open grassy knoll and becomes somewhat indistinct. Nonetheless, if you stay aware of the rock cairns marking the route, there is little danger of losing your way.

During April of 1993 when we hiked this trail, the agave were sending skyward their giant spears, looking much like enormous 4-inch wide asparagus shoots. We noted in this vicinity a large collared lizard, a brilliant iridescent green in the morning sunlight. Some of the wildflowers of note at these lower elevations included verbena, Indian paintbrush, filaree, and wild onion.

At about 1 mile, as the trail descends to George Wood Canyon, you will encounter a mutilated wilderness boundary sign. Rather than human vandalism, this sign had been chewed on by black bears.

The trail now takes the form of an old 8-foot wide roadway. Staying close the canyon bottom, the trail follows a shaded route under cover of giant old-growth junipers and pines.

At about 1.6 miles the trail leaves the canyon and begins a series of steep switchbacks to the Juniper Mesa rim. Just below the rim we encountered the first of a series of bear scats, loaded with juniper berries.

At mile 2.0 you will come to a wire gate and, just east of the gate, a trail sign. The sign says that the direction to Pine Spring (Trail #3 terminus) goes south from here, a distance of 3 miles. Someone in an apparent attempt to mislead, has carved a small arrow in the sign pointing north. The trail south toward the rim now follows an old road. This is pleasant hiking here beneath an open stand of old yellowbark ponderosa pines, Gambel oak, and alligator junipers. More bear scats were seen along this road.

Within 0.7 miles you will come to another faded trail sign. This is a critical junction. The trail straight ahead goes to Juniper Spring, a distance of 6 miles. Though not named on the sign, this is the Juniper Mesa Trail #20. Our trail turns left here to Pine Spring, a distance of 2 more miles. Again, someone has scratched over the existing sign and scratched in arrows reversing the directions. This is a dangerous bit of vandalism. This is too big a country in which to get lost or confused, particularly if not equipped for several days of camping. Ignore the editing on these signs.

Trail #3 from here begins a gradual descent within a generally shaded canyon along an old road to Pine Spring and Forest Road 7.

If you wish to make this a loop trip using the Juniper Mesa Trail #20 and the Juniper Spring Trail #2, see the separate descriptions for those trails. Be aware, however, that from the aforementioned gate, the total distance along Trail #20 and Trail #2 to FR 150 is about 9.5 miles.

For perhaps the only easy hiking within the Juniper Mesa Wilderness, approach Trail #3 from the north on FR 7. Follow the two-track road past the wilderness boundary in a very gradual ascent in the Pine Creek drainage to Juniper Mesa Rim, a distance of about 2 miles.

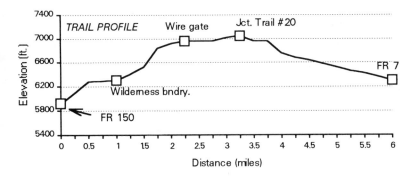

JUNIPER MESA TRAIL #20
JUNIPER SPRINGS TRAIL #2
OAKS & WILLOWS TRAIL #3

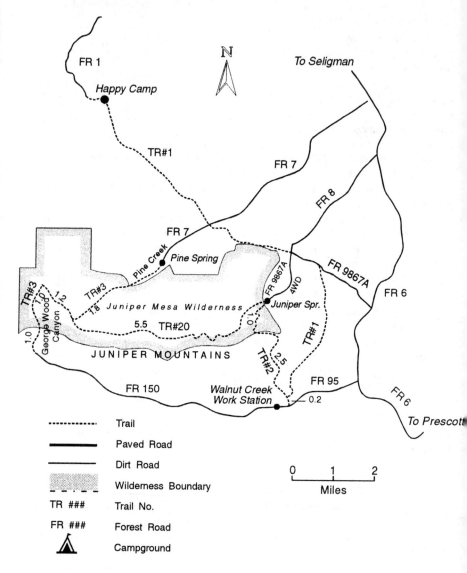

N

FR 1

Happy Camp

To Seligman

TR#1

FR 7

FR 8

FR 7

Pine Creek

Pine Spring

FR 9867A

4WD

FR 9867A

FR 6

TR#3

TR#3

1.2

Juniper Mesa Wilderness

Juniper Spr.

George Wood Canyon

1.0

.7

1.0

.8

5.5   TR#20

0.1

TR#1

JUNIPER MOUNTAINS

TR#2

2.5

FR 150

Walnut Creek Work Station

FR 95

FR 6

0.2

To Prescott

....	Trail
▬▬▬▬	Paved Road
————	Dirt Road
▨▨▨▨	Wilderness Boundary
TR ###	Trail No.
FR ###	Forest Road
⛺	Campground

0   1   2
Miles

HYDE MOUNTAIN TRAIL #6

General information:

This trail is primarily a service trail to Hyde Mountain Lookout, but is always open to hikers. Hyde Mountain at the fire lookout is 7,272 feet in elevation. Being the highest point in the Santa Maria Mountains, it offers excellent vistas of the Santa Maria Mountains and much of northern Arizona.

The lookout is listed in the National Register of Historic Places as an historic example of CCC era construction. Rather than sitting atop a steel frame tower, it is actually a 12 foot by 12 foot wooden house, and is the only one of this style within the Prescott National Forest. The house retains most of its original design, construction materials, and is still on the site where it was built.

Access and trailhead location: Map: p. 80

From downtown Prescott drive north on Montezuma St. for 1.7 miles to the 4-way intersection. Continue west on Iron Springs Rd. to Williamson Valley Road. Turn north (right) on Williamson Valley Rd. and continue for approximately 22 miles to the turnoff to Camp Wood (FR 21). It is then 16 miles more to Camp Wood. Turn north on FR 95 for about 0.3 miles. Turn west on FR 95C and go approximately 1.7 miles to the trailhead near the end of this road. Vehicle parking here is limited, as is turn-around space.

Road condition: Paved to FR 21 (Camp Wood Rd.), then dirt, but suitable for all vehicles when dry.

Hiking time: 1.5 hours   *Length:* 2 miles, one-way.

Difficulty: Difficult because of the steep ascent and lack of water.

Use: Moderate.

Uses permitted: The entire trail is a primitive or semi-primitive road and motorized transportation is permitted.

Recommended seasons of use: spring, summer, fall

Maps, other resources: Prescott National Forest, west half; U.S.G.S. topographic 7.5′ quad for Camp Wood.

Trail description:

The trail climbs directly to the lookout on Hyde Mountain. The latter third of the trail is steep and difficult. The trail branches about 0.25 miles south of the lookout. This fork descends to the west for about 0.8 miles and joins the Brown Springs Trail #5 just northeast of the saddle between Hyde Mountain and Pinetop Mountain.

Caution: This can be a hot, difficult climb. Take frequent breaks and carry plenty of drinking water; none is available on the trail or at the lookout on Hyde Mountain.

HYDE MOUNTAIN TRAIL #6

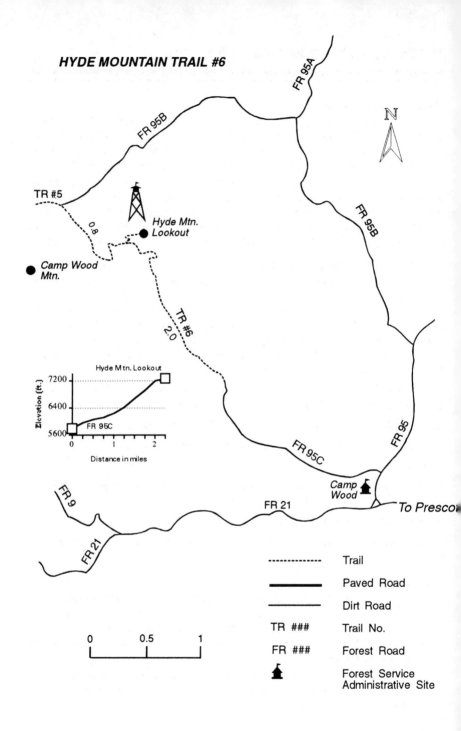

FR 95A

N

FR 95B

TR #5

0.8

Hyde Mtn.
Lookout

Camp Wood
Mtn.

FR 95B

TR #6

2.0

Hyde Mtn. Lookout

7200

6400

5600

FR 95C

0   1   2

Distance in miles

FR 95C

FR 95

Camp
Wood

To Prescot

FR 9

FR 21

FR 21

----------	Trail
----------	Paved Road
----------	Dirt Road
TR ###	Trail No.
FR ###	Forest Road
▲	Forest Service Administrative Site

0   0.5   1

Mingus Mountain

WITH ITS COMMANDING VIEW OF LONESOME VALLEY to the west and the Verde Valley to the east, Mingus Mountain is a popular destination for Arizona residents and tourists. Its 7,500 foot elevation and cool summer temperatures attract overheated valley residents from the Phoenix area, Prescott, and the Verde Valley.

A 24-unit campground is just 4 miles in from Highway 89A on dirt road. It is from here that most of the areas trails are reached. The road into the campground area is closed to vehicular traffic and locked during winter and may not open until well into May. In late winter or spring, hikers wishing to reach the trails leaving the Mingus rim must walk an additional 2 miles from the gate just to reach the trailheads.

A number of trails, however, can be approached from Allen Springs Road (FR 413) which circles the mountain at about the 6,800-foot level. This access provides for any number of one-way or round-trip hikes or rides even during winter when snow lies deep on the Woodchute and Mingus mesas.

The fire tower near the Methodist Camp may be of interest to history buffs. The 7-foot by 7-foot cab atop the 59-foot steel tower was erected in 1935. Apparently nothing of significance has been done to either this tower, its cab, or adjoining cabin to alter their original design. Because of this and their 50-year plus age, these structures have been recommended for inclusion in the National Register of Historic Places.

The geology of this region adds another dimension to the exploration of Woodchute and Mingus Mountains. Faulting and uplift of layers of stratified rock have brought massive ore bodies close to the surface in many parts of the eastern slopes of Mingus. Jerome and its once rich mining district lie within one of these exposed areas. However, a thick layer of basalt caps the summit of Mingus. Below the basalt are layers of first sandstone, then limestones that may be several hundred feet thick and contain upper Devonian era fossils. These limestone outcroppings are most obvious on trails that descend the west side of Mingus.

Just a few miles east of the Mingus summit on Highway 89A lies the town of Jerome and its mining district. Now home to a population of mainly artists, artisans, and shopkeepers, Jerome is a pleasant place in which to explore. At dusk watch the shadows lengthen across the valley below, then end your day in one of its many tiny restaurants.

COLEMAN TRAIL #108

General information:

This trail leaves the Mingus Mountain campground area in the vicinity of the radio facilities at the south end of the mesa top. From there it goes in a southeast direction, staying close to the edge of the Mingus rim. There are some wonderful views from this rim of the Cottonwood area and the entire Verde Valley.

Trail #108 can also be used as part of a loop route that begins and ends on FR 104A. You can descend on Trail #108, walk west on the Allen Springs Road for 0.6 miles, and then return to the rim by way of Trail #9037 which goes up Gaddes Canyon. The total distance is approximately 5.5 miles. The combination of these two trails provides the hiker with a diverse experience — broad vistas from the Mingus rim to a cool forested canyon walk.

Access and trailhead location: Map: p. 102

To reach the north end of the trail, travel north from downtown Prescott on Highway 89 then east on Highway 89A for a total distance of about 25 miles. At the summit north of Mingus Mountain, take Forest Road 104 south for approximately 2.6 miles to the Mingus Mountain campground. At the campground turn right and continue south through the camping areas for 0.7 miles to a point almost opposite the radio facilities. There is a spur road to the right just as you pass under some power lines. The trailhead and sign for Trail #108 is just a few yards down this road.

Road condition: FR 104 and 104A are dirt but suitable for all vehicles when they are dry and free of snow.

Hiking time: 1 hour   *Length:* 1.8 miles.

Difficulty: Moderate   *Use:* Moderate.

Uses permitted: Hiking, horseback riding, and bicycles (non-motorized) are permitted. However, loose rock on the steep switchbacks of this trail render it unsuitable for any but the most experienced horseback riders.

Recommended seasons of use: spring, summer, fall

Maps, other resources: Prescott National Forest, west half; U.S.G.S. topographic 7.5′ quad for Cottonwood.

Trail description:

From the trailhead near the radio facilities the trail heads in a generally southeast direction along the Mingus rim. About 50 yards down this 4WD road you will come to a routed-wood sign showing that Trail #108 leaves this road to the left (east).

At 0.3 miles the trail again returns to the road as it descends along a slight gradient to the southeast. There are some good views to the south. The vegetation along this section of the rim is an open park-like stand of ponderosa pine, scattered alligator junipers, and clumps of Gambel oak.

At 0.7 miles the old roadbed becomes a narrow trail. In the spring of 1993 when we hiked this route we saw several brilliant yellow, red, and black western tanagers. Hummingbirds also seemed to be abundant, though we did not identify them. The south-facing end of this mesa is drier and warmer than many areas on the mesa top. The agave were sending up their 4-inch wide shoots and hedgehog cacti were capped with tight clusters of brilliant red flowers.

At 1.3 miles the trail descends in earnest. The surface of the trail is very loose and rocky, making it dangerous for horseback use. Even the footing is treacherous.

At 2.0 miles you will reach the Allen Springs Road (FR 413). If you continue west from here you have several options. At 0.6 miles there are two trailheads. The first one is Trail #9037 at Gaddes Canyon. This trail goes directly up Gaddes Canyon in a northwest direction. It stays in the canyon bottom for about 1.8 miles and then climbs to the northeast for about another mile to FR 104A, joining that road just a few yards north of the trailhead for Trail #108. This would make a good loop route of about 5.5 miles.

Just a few yards west of the sign for Trail #9037 is one for Trail #114, the Black Canyon Trail. This latter trail goes almost due south down Gaddes Canyon for one mile to where it joins Black Canyon. The trail stays in Black Canyon for a short distance and then heads east to Quail Springs, ending at FR 359. Trail #114 combined with Trail #108 provides a route of over 8.5 miles that descends over 3,400 feet in elevation to the desert floor. It would be a good cool season trip if you could arrange to be picked up from the Cottonwood area.

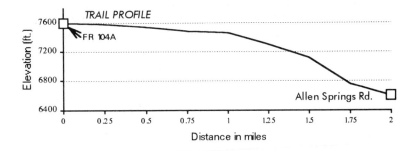

GADDES CANYON TRAIL #9037

General information:

The name listed for this trail within the Forest Service database of trails information is "Gaddes 2." I have taken the liberty of renaming this the Gaddes Canyon Trail. The trail draws all of its attributes from the magnificence of this canyon and travels for almost its entire length within the canyon bottom. The official "Gaddes Canyon Trail #110" merely crosses Gaddes Canyon near Gaddes Spring. Consequently, I have called this latter trail the Gaddes Spring Trail #110, thus holding to the original trail number but renaming it to better describe where it goes.

Gaddes Canyon drains Mingus Mountain to the southeast, carving deeply through the layered rock for about four miles. It is a jewel of a place, contrasting sharply with the dry, brush covered slopes on either side of the canyon. Far below the southeast ledges of Mingus it is a deeply shadowed ephemeral stream course that sustains a lush growth of mammoth ponderosa pines, Arizona walnuts, boxelder, and the ever present New Mexico locust. Besides an occasional glimpse of the rocky bluffs above, there are no panoramic views from the trail itself. Only when you reach the summit of Mingus and walk the short distance to the east rim are you rewarded with the wonderful panoramas of the Verde Valley and the Oak Creek area.

Densely vegetated canyons such as this support much of the wildlife of the region: black bears, mule deer, mountain lion, wild turkeys, and javelina, to mention just the largest species.

Access and trailhead location: Map: p. 102

To reach the south end of the trail, travel north from downtown Prescott on Highway 89 then east on Highway 89A for a total distance of about 25 miles. At the road summit on Mingus Mountain there is a paved turnoff to the right (south) to the Methodist Camp. Take this road (FR 104) for 1.3 miles to where it intersects with FR 413. Take FR 413 west, then south, then east. At a distance of 3 miles from the FR 413/FR 104 junction you will pass the trailhead for the Gaddes Canyon Trail #110 on the left of the road. This is the trail that I have renamed the Gaddes Spring Trail. Then at mile 5.8 miles you will reach the trailhead for Trail #114 and the ample parking areas within this shaded canyon. This is where Gaddes Canyon crosses FR 413 (Allen Springs Rd.). The trailhead for Trail #9037 is just a few yards east of the parking area.

To reach the north trailhead, follow the directions outlined above as far as the FR 104/FR 413 junction. Instead of turning right here, continue on FR 104 for another 1.3 miles to the Mingus Mountain campground. At the campground turn right and continue south through the camping areas for 0.7 miles to a point almost opposite the radio facilities. There is a spur road to the right just as you pass under some power lines. Two signs mark this road: the trail sign for Trail #9037 and another showing the road closure.

Road condition: Dirt on the Allen Springs Road but suitable for all vehicles

Hiking time: 2.5 hours   *Length:* 3 miles

Difficulty: Easy   *Use:* Moderate

Uses permitted: Hiking and horseback riding only.

Recommended seasons of use: spring, summer, fall

Maps, other resources: Prescott National Forest, east half; U.S.G.S. topographic 7.5′ quads for Hickey Mountain and Cottonwood.

Trail description:

I will describe this trail from the Allen Springs Road to the campground area on Mingus. The trail begins along an old roadbed, traveling among gigantic ponderosa pines that line either side of Gaddes Canyon. These huge yellow-bark pines apparently benefit from the moist canyon bottom to achieve such large diameters. The lushness of the canyon belies the fact that the creek in late June, 1993, when we hiked it, was completely dry. At mile 0.3 the road ends and a narrow brush-covered trail continues along the east side of the creek.

The trail here is almost jungle-like. The newer growth of thickets of New Mexico locust encroaches on the path and makes hikers force their way through its low-growing branches. With the trail in its present condition, I would not recommend wearing shorts. One member of our party did so when we last hiked it and was rewarded with a mosaic of scratches on calves and thighs.

The trail, though, was really a delight to hike. It is deeply padded with pine needles and oak leaves and ascends gradually. There are, however, a couple of cautions worth noting. This warm, moist canyon bottom has produced an abundance of poison ivy that in many places encroaches on the path. Also, the dense vegetation bordering the path limits visibility to either side. Be sure of your footing and be wary of the possible presence of rattlesnakes.

There are a rich variety of wildflowers in Gaddes Canyon. The flowering will depend, of course, on the season. On this early summer day we saw wild roses, yellow columbine, wild geraniums, and New Mexico locust. The brilliant red penstemon, sometimes called the scarlet bugler, was also abundant. The New Mexico raspberry, a very tall rangy shrub, had already produced berries. In spring this is a very showy plant with large white five-petaled flowers.

At mile 1.2 the trail climbs about 50 feet above the west bank of the canyon. From here you get a rare view of the Mingus rim.

The trail crosses the canyon bottom often. It is at these crossings that you need to stay alert to where the trail exits the rocky creek bed. Be assured, however, that within the first 1.8 miles this trail never strays more than a few feet from a course parallel to the canyon bottom.

At mile 1.7 a huge ponderosa pine, long dead, lies straight across the canyon bottom. The trail detours around this log on the east side, but then within just a few yards, crosses to the west side.

Then at mile 2.0 there is a critical trail junction. Another large pine, lying parallel to the creek on the east side, marks this spot. A large rock sits atop the cut end of this log. Here the trail to the top of Mingus heads east, marked only with a few rock cairns. The left fork of the trail stays within the canyon, continuing for another 0.75 miles to Gaddes Spring and a junction with Trail #110.

The fork to the Mingus rim climbs steeply at first along a narrow, rocky path. It soon becomes more gradual as it reaches the rim, passing over bare volcanic ledges. Be alert to the 2 or 3-rock cairns marking the trail route where it crosses some open rocky areas.

At mile 2.6 the trail follows a rocky primitive road, long since closed to vehicular traffic. Dirt berms have been built across the road to deter vehicles. Huge boulders have also been pushed into strategic spots. All of this makes for rough walking or bicycling along this short stretch of road. The trail then passes a cattle tank on the right and then ends on FR 401A just 0.5 miles south of the main campground area on Mingus Mountain.

Tip! For a round-trip of 6.0 miles that begins and ends on Mingus Mountain, descend on the Coleman Trail #108 to the Allen Springs Road (FR 413). Then take the road west for 0.5 miles, and return to the Mingus rim via Trail #9037. You will end just about 400 yards north of where you started near the radio towers and antennas.

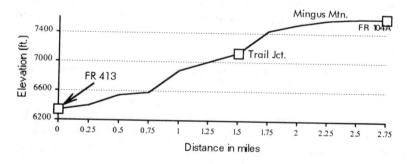

GADDES SPRING TRAIL #110

General information:

This trail is popular with campers on Mingus Mountain because it provides an easy day hike from the campground to the points overlooking Gaddes Canyon. The hike down into the cool moist canyon itself is well worth the extra mile, however. Springs seeping from the east slope of the canyon feed a lush and rich variety of plants that occur just above the point where the trail crosses the canyon floor.

The rest of the trail stays primarily in the ponderosa pine and Gambel oak vegetation types and, consequently, is a pleasant shaded route for almost its entire length. Because the route stays within a forest canopy, there are not many viewing points. An exception is the edge of the rim before the trail drops down to Allen Springs Road (FR 413).

Access and trailhead location: Map: p. 102

To reach the north end of the trail, travel north from downtown Prescott on Highway 89 then east on Highway 89A for a total distance of about 25 miles. At the summit north of Mingus Mountain take Forest Road 104 (to Methodist Camp) south for approximately 2 miles toward the Mingus Mountain campground area. Just as you pass the last building on the site of the Methodist Camp turn right on FR 104B (lookout road) and drive for 0.2 miles to the trailhead sign for Trail #110.

To reach the south trailhead, turn south on FR 104 from Hwy. 89A and drive for 1.3 miles to the intersection with FR 413 (Allen Springs Rd.). Turn right (west) here and continue on this road for 3.0 miles to the trailhead for Trail #110 on the left of the road.

Road condition: FR 413 is dirt, but suitable for all vehicles when the road is not muddy or snow covered.

Hiking time: 2.5 hours.   *Length:* 3 miles.

Difficulty: Moderate.   *Use:* Moderate.

Uses permitted: Hiking and horseback riding only.

Recommended seasons of use: spring, summer, fall

Maps, other resources: Prescott National Forest, east half; U.S.G.S. topographic 7.5′ quad for Hickey Mountain.

Trail description:

I will describe this route starting on FR 413. The lower part of the trail is quite wide as it follows an old roadbed. It is a pleasant walk or ride here as it travels through an open stand of ponderosa pines and small groves of Gambel oak. After about 0.3 miles the trail begins to climb more steeply and rough lava rock comprises the trail surface.

At 0.4 miles the trail turns sharply right, away from the road that it had been following. This is a critical junction marked only by a pile of lava rock on each side of the trail. Another good landmark for this junction is a yellow, very resinous 25-foot tall pine snag that stands within a few feet of the junction.

At 1.1 miles you will come to a trail sign for Trail #110. At this point the trail follows a road (FR 9003N) to the northeast. The sign marks the point at which the trail leaves this road when you are traveling the trail from north to south. You will travel along this road for about 0.5 miles before encountering another sign for Trail #110. At this point the trail again leaves the road on an azimuth of about 20 degrees and becomes much narrower. You will soon be on the east slope of the ridge and will begin a steady descent to Gaddes Canyon.

At 1.9 miles you will reach the lush canyon bottom. In spring and summer wild irises carpet the wet stream channel and wild roses grow on the east slope of the canyon, fed by water seeping down from Gaddes Spring. It is worth exploring upstream from where the trail crosses the canyon. On this trip I noted a pair of solitary vireos flitting among the wet moss-covered rocks of the canyon bottom. The trail then leaves the canyon, climbing through a set of switchbacks past Gaddes Spring.

At 2.5 miles the trail intersects a road. This intersection is marked by a large of pile of rocks to alert the southbound traveler that the trail leaves the road at this point. Follow this road northeast another quarter-mile to a wire gate and trail sign. From the gate it is just 0.2 miles north to the lookout tower road, and another 0.2 miles back to FR 104 and the Methodist Camp.

Solitary Vireo

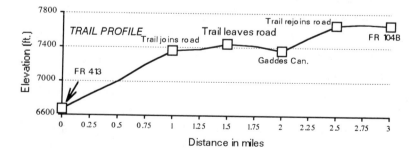

MINGUS MOUNTAIN

NORTH MINGUS TRAIL #105

General information:

This trail, used in combination with TR #106 and TR #105A, makes an attractive loop route, allowing day trips that return to the Mingus Mountain campground area. This is also a good trail for arranging to have vehicles at both ends of the trail, one at the campground and the other on FR 338 at Mescal Spring. This is a particularly attractive trail during the fall because of the changing colors of the many small pockets of aspen and other deciduous trees on the north side of Mingus Mountain. The bigtooth maple, in particular, turns to a billiant red in the fall. From east facing portions of this trail you can also get nice views of Jerome, Cottonwood, and the Verde Valley. From the point where the trail descends the Mingus rim, there are wonderful views to the northeast of Sycamore Canyon and the mountain peaks in the Williams-Flagstaff area.

In the spring, and particularly in early May, this trail is spectacular for its display of blooming shrubs and a great variety of wildflowers.

Access and trailhead location: Map: p. 102

To reach the north end of the trail, travel north from downtown Prescott on Highway 89 then east on Highway 89A for a total distance of about 25 miles. At the summit north of Mingus Mountain, take Forest Road 104 south for approximately 2.6 miles to the Mingus Mountain campground. At the campground take the left fork road for about 0.7 miles to the hang glider site where the trailhead is located. There is a nice turn-around and parking space here and a vault toilet.

The north trailhead is reached from Highway 89A at Mescal Tank. Coming from the Prescott area, the wide highway turnoff to FR 338 is just 2.9 miles east of the summit of Mingus. You will recognize the wide pulloff from the highway since it is just east of the sign showing that you are entering the Prescott National Forest when approaching this sign from Jerome. The trailhead on FR 338 is not marked by a sign, but is approximately 2 miles along FR 338 from Hwy. 89A. FR 338 is passable to high-clearance vehicles. Be alert as you approach this trail since there is no sign to mark the trail, only crudely constructed rock cairns.

Road condition: The dirt road (FR 104) to the campground from Hwy. 89A is suitable for all vehicles provided that it is dry and free of snow. If you plan to visit the campground area in early spring, check with the Verde Valley District office at (602) 567-4121 to make sure that the road to the campground past the turnoff to FR 413 is open. The roadway to the campground beyond this point remains snow-covered and muddy much longer than the approach road from Hwy 89A and its opening may be delayed well into May.

Hiking time: 3 hours   *Length:* 5.3 miles to Hwy. 89A.

Difficulty: Moderate   *Use:* Moderate

Uses permitted: Hiking and horseback riding only.

Recommended seasons of use: spring, summer, fall

Maps, other resources: Prescott National Forest, east half; U.S.G.S. topographic 7.5′ quads for Cottonwood and Hickey Mountain.

Trail description:

The pleasure of this trail begins immediately at the trailhead on the Mingus rim. It leaves just past the hang glider ramp. The view of the Verde Valley from this ramp is spectacular. The trail then travels through an attractive open, park-like forest of ponderosa pine towards the north end of the rim. The trail along or close to the rim is not always obvious. One needs to pay attention to the numerous rock cairns marking the route.

Along this section of trail, prior to descending to the north, you will see one of the most beautiful trees of the central mountain region — the white fir. You will recognize it from its silvery bark, long (2in.) and soft blue-green upcurved needles.

At 0.6 miles you will reach a dramatic section of trail at the point where it plunges from the Mingus rim. There are spectacular views to the north from here. On an azimuth of 360 deg. is Woodchute Mountain lying within the Woodchute Wilderness. Beyond this point the trail begins a series of switchbacks that cross numerous small drainages. It is this contouring route that makes this trail so attractive as its passes through the small stands of aspen and oak that occupy the cool mountain drainages that descend the north slope of Mingus Mtn. These switchbacks also give considerable relief to the steep slope whether ascending or descending.

There are some interesting plants to note along the higher portions of the trail. There are plants here that I have not encountered along other trails in the Prescott area. Particularly abundant is Utah serviceberry. It has a 5-petaled white flower with sepals that turn down. The canyon drainages are thick with shrubby bigtooth maples. Thickets of fragrant ash, white-blossomed New Mexico raspberry, and Fendlerbush occupy the more open slopes. This latter shrub, when is full

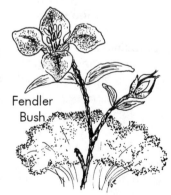

Fendler Bush

bloom and covered with its 1-inch white blossoms, is particularly spectacular. You will recognize it for its 4-petaled white flower, the petals of which open widely separated. It reminds me of the blossom of the unrelated eastern dogwood tree.

At about 1.3 miles you will reach the junction with Trail #105A. This is the connector to Trail #106 which descends the east side of Mingus. The distance to Trail #106 is probably closer to 0.7 miles than the 0.5 miles indicated by the sign. The other two signs direct you along Trail #105 either back to the top of Mingus or to FR 338. The mileage to Mescal Gulch on FR 338 is 2 miles.

Just prior to reaching these signs it is worth noting the beautiful iridescent yellow-green lichens that occur on the rocks along the trail.

Some other flowers in abundance in spring along the middle sections of this trail are the blue flax, pink phlox, and western wallflower.

You will soon enter a limestone area where the footing becomes more difficult over the limestone cobble. This is also a drier site as evidenced by the occurence of pinyon pines. Then, as you cross a couple of cool canyons, you will find maples, Douglas firs, and Gambel oaks in the first of these — a great spot for a lunch or rest break. It is in this vicinity that the trail offers a chance to look back at the north face of Mingus and marvel at the mosaic of vegetation that makes this trail so enjoyable.

At about 2.5 miles the trail intersects with FR 338. Turn left (west) here and follow the road for about 2 miles to its junction with Hwy. 89A.

Tip!

Hike or ride this trail in combination with Trail #106 and Trail #105A. If you do so, I would recommend that you hike down Trail #106, north across Trail #105A, and return to the Mingus rim via Trail #105. In this way you will ascend on the gentle switchbacks of Trail #105 at the end of your trip. Trail #106 is extremely steep and rocky. This is a total of 4 miles on these trails, but there is an additional 0.7 mile walk on roads back to the trailhead for Trail #106 at the campground.

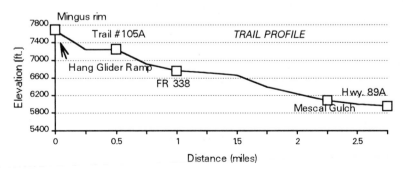

LITTLE YEAGER TRAIL #111

General information:

This trail is used mainly as a connection between Trail #28 and Trail #533, thus creating a possible round-trip loop back to the trailheads on Highway 89A. The trail goes north-south staying mainly in a ponderosa pine forest. It is a very pleasant trail that stays for most of its length within or close to the cool drainage of Little Yeager Canyon. Consequently, there are no vista points.

Access and trailhead location: Map: p. 102

To reach the north end of the trail, travel east from downtown Prescott on Highway 89A for a distance of about 25 miles. At the road summit on Mingus Mountain there is a paved turnoff to the right (south) to the Methodist Camp. Take this road (FR 104) for 1.3 miles to where it intersects with FR 413. Take FR 413 west for 0.8 miles to the trailhead for Trail #28.

To reach the south trailhead, instead of taking TR #28, continue driving south on FR 413 for an additional 1.4 miles to the junction with FR 132. Then take FR 132 southwest for 0.4 miles to the junction with FR 105. Take FR 105 west for 0.25 miles to the trailhead for TR #111.

To use this trail as part of a loop from Trail #28 to Trail #111 to Trail #533, you would probably want to start at the Highway 89A access to Trail #28. The directions to that trailhead are as follows: Instead of going to the Mingus summit, at 21.6 miles from downtown Prescott there is a dirt road turnoff from Highway 89A on the south side of the highway. This turnoff is just 1.4 miles past the point where you pass beneath the twin power transmission lines on Highway 89A. The trailhead for Trail #28 will be on your left just below the highway. To locate the trailhead for Trail #533, continue past the trailhead for Trail #28 for only about 0.1 miles, crossing a cattle guard to a grove of ash trees and old foundations. The trailhead is just to the south of this clearing.

Road condition: The dirt access roads are suitable for all vehicles when they are dry and free of snow.

Hiking time: 1.5 hours   *Length:* 2 miles

Difficulty: Easy   *Use:* Moderate

Uses permitted: Hiking, horseback riding; no bicycles are permitted.

Recommended seasons of use: spring, summer, fall

Maps, other resources: Prescott National Forest, east half; U.S.G.S. topographic 7.5′ quad for Hickey Mountain.

Trail description:

I will describe this trail starting at the east trailhead for Trail #28. As you travel west from the parking area on Trail #28 you will soon come to a fenced area enclosing a concrete apron and water catchment basin. This is a device for collecting rain and storing it in a small basin that is accessible to wildlife. The trail here is nicely maintained with many erosion control logs placed across the trail. In this section the trail travels under a canopy of second growth ponderosa pine.

At 0.4 miles you will come to an old routed-wood sign showing a distance of 2 miles to Highway 89A. Beneath this sign is another pointing south to Trail #111, a distance of 2 miles to Mud Flat. Turn south at this point.

For the first few yards this trail travels an old roadbed, now closed to vehicular traffic. There were lots of deer tracks along here when we last hiked it. Since this part of the route is on a dry west-facing slope, alligator juniper and a scattering of agave (century plants) dominate the vegetation.

At 0.5 miles be alert. You will encounter another routed-wood sign indicating that Trail #111 goes to the right. As you turn you will immediately see the newer vertical fiberglass sign for Trail #111.

At 0.8 miles the trail begins a series of sharp switchbacks to the bottom of Little Yeager Canyon, passing an attractive grove of Gambel oaks just before reaching the canyon bottom.

At 1.0 miles the trail is still paralleling the canyon but on the eastern slope above the creek. There is a rough section of trail here that requires caution. Heavy rains during the winter of 1993 used this trail as a waterway, scouring away the loose trail surface, thus making walking a little difficult.

At about 1.4 miles the trail is quite level again and easy walking as it begins to angle away from Little Yeager Canyon. It also enters a drier, warmer site.

At 1.8 miles the trail descends to a south facing slope and into a much more open pine stand. This site features lots of large Arizona white oaks. Distinguish this oak from the Emory oak (both evergreen oaks) by the color and shape of its leaves. The leaves of the white oak are broader and less serrated than those of the Emory oak. Their color is also a dull bluish-green as opposed to the more shiny bright green of the Emory oak leaves.

At 2.4 miles the trail climbs to a little knoll after crossing a small southeast tributary of Little Yeager Canyon. Finally, at about 2.6 miles you will encounter a cattle gate, and just beyond that a fiberglass trail marker.

To continue to Trail #533, take the dirt road west from here for about 0.2 miles to a large highway sign. Just to the right of this sign is the smaller vertical sign for Trail #533.

Although we were not diligently searching for birds when we hiked this trail, we saw many mountain chickadees and white-breasted nuthatches. The trail surface was frequently marked by tracks of coyotes and deer.

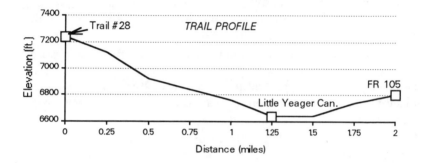

Mountain Chickadee

YEAGER CABIN TRAIL #533

General information:

This trail is part of a system of trails that can be used as a round-trip loop. Starting at one of two trailheads on Highway 89A, one can take either Trail #28 or Trail #533 to the east. Make the return trip by way of the connecting trail, TR #111. Since this trail descends the steep west face of Mingus Mountain, there are some spectacular views to the west of the northern Bradshaw Mountains, Granite Mountain, the mountains near Camp Wood, and the Juniper Mesa area. In late spring and particularly in late summer, if the rainfall has been adequate, the expanse of verdant grass in valleys to the west of Mingus can be a stunning sight indeed.

Access and trailhead location: Map: p. 102

To use the east trailhead, travel east from Prescott on Highway 89A for approximately 25 miles to the summit north of Mingus Mountain. Drive south on the paved (only for short distance) road to the Methodist Camp (FR 104) for approximately 1.3 miles to where it intersects with FR 413. Drive west on FR 413 for 0.8 miles and then south for another 1.4 miles to the junction with FR 132. Take FR 132 southwest to the junction with FR 105. Then drive west on FR 105 west for just 0.4 miles past the trail sign for Trail #111 to the trail sign for Trail #533.

Road condition: All of the dirt access roads to this trail are suitable for all vehicles if the roads are dry and free of snow.

Hiking time: 1.5 hours   *Length:* 2.2 miles

Difficulty: Easy to difficult depending on direction of travel

Use: Moderate

Uses permitted: Hiking, horseback riding. No bicycles are permitted.

Recommended seasons of use: all seasons, except that the access roads on Mingus may be closed or impassable during winter.

Maps, other resources: Prescott National Forest, east half; U.S.G.S. topographic 7.5' quad for Hickey Mountain.

Trail description:

We will describe this trail from east to west. The first part of the trail is across rough limestone rock, though easy to follow. It climbs a slight rise through a very open stand of brush, agave (century plant), and scattered junipers and pinyon pines. Within a short distance the trail reaches the edge of this limestone ledge and descends to the northwest.

You are immediately rewarded to the west with some truly magnificent views of Chino Valley and Granite Mountain (azimuth = 270 deg.).

More vistas open as you move down the trail a short distance. At 0.4 miles you get a wonderful view of the northern Bradshaw Mountains. If you are not familiar with the landmarks, Mt. Union at nearly 8,000 feet in elevation is on an azimuth of 214 degrees. Towers Mountain is at 200 degrees, Mt. Tritle at 220 degrees, and Prescott Valley area at about 256 degrees.

At 0.6 miles the trail descends through some loose lava rock. Be particularly careful here as these rounded lava rocks will tend to roll beneath your feet. Vegetation here on this warm south-facing slope is very tall brush of 6 to 8 feet, mostly mountain mahogany and silk tassel. Pinyon pine is the dominant tree. The year 1993, when we hiked this trail, featured an abundant crop of cones on both pinyon and ponderosa pines. The trails were literally covered with cones in places. Larger ponderosa cones, like the lava rocks, can also be a little hazardous to hikers as they tend to roll underfoot.

At 0.9 the trail begins a series of switchbacks, passing through another zone of limestone. This rock, in contrast to the dark gray limestone at the beginning of the trail, is stark white, loose and broken.

At 2.1 miles just before reaching the trailhead sign, the trail widens to a road. The trailhead sign is then just 0.1 miles farther and just south of a large clearing. This clearing features a nice grove of mostly ash trees amid foundations of a former habitation.

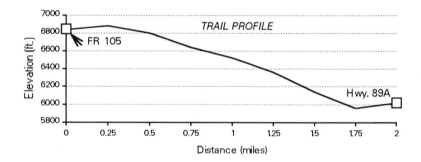

YEAGER CANYON TRAIL #28

General information:

This trail on the west slope of Mingus Mountain offers fine views of Lonesome Valley, Prescott Valley area, and Bradshaw Mountains. The trail starts in ponderosa pine but at elevations below the rim stays mostly in pinyon pine and juniper. An attractive riparian vegetation type and associated deciduous hardwoods occurs in the 0.7 miles of the portion of the trail that parallels Highway 89A in Yeager Canyon. This trail is in good condition, having been repaired during 1990.

The trail is a portion of a system of trails that can be used as a round-trip loop, a total distance of approximately 7 miles. Starting at either of the trailheads on Highway 89A, one can take Trail #28 or Trail #533 to the east. Return by way of the connecting trail, Trail #111.

Access and trailhead location: Map: p. 102

To reach the west end of the trail, travel east from downtown Prescott on Hwy. 89A for 21.6 miles. There is a dirt road turnoff from Highway 89A on the south side of the highway, just 1.4 miles past the point where you pass beneath the twin power transmission lines on Highway 89A. The trailhead for Trail #28 will be on your left just below the highway.

To reach the east end of the trail, travel to the summit of Mingus Mountain, 3.5 miles farther east from the previous turnoff. At the road summit on Mingus Mountain take the paved turnoff to the right (south) to the Methodist Camp. Follow this road (FR 104) for 1.3 miles to where it intersects with FR 413. Take FR 413 west for 0.8 miles to the trailhead for Trail #28.

Road condition: All dirt access roads to this trail are suitable for all types of vehicles when the roads are dry and free of snow.

Hiking time: 1.5 hours   *Length:* 2.3 miles

Difficulty: Difficult to moderate depending on direction of travel

Use: Moderate

Uses permitted: Hiking and horseback riding only

Recommended season of use: All seasons, although the access roads on Mingus Mountain may be closed in winter due to snow.

Maps, other resources: Prescott National Forest, east half; U.S.G.S. topographic 7.5′ quad for Hickey Mountain.

Trail description:

I will describe this trail starting at the east trailhead for Trail #28. As you travel west from the parking area for Trail #28 you will soon come to a fenced area enclosing a concrete apron and water catchment basin. This is a device for collecting rain and storing it in a small basin that is accessible to wildlife. The trail here is nicely maintained with many erosion control logs placed across the trail. In this section the trail travels under a canopy of second growth ponderosa pine.

At 0.3 miles you will come to a routed-wood sign indicating a distance of 2 miles to Highway 89A. Beneath this sign is another pointing south to Trail #111. It shows a distance of 2 miles to Mud Flat. Continue west from this point.

At 0.5 miles, near a large alligator juniper, there is a fine overlook. If you look on an azimuth of about 210 degrees you will see the highest point in the Bradshaw Mountains, Mt. Union, at an elevation of almost 8,000 feet. If you look to the right of this mountain but along the same ridge, you will see the fire tower atop Spruce Mountain. Despite its name, there are no spruce trees in this region. The beautiful white fir, locally abundant in the Bradshaws, may have been misidentified by some early pioneer.

From this point the trail begins a rapid descent of the mountain, traversing a brushy slope that faces roughly south-southeast and overlooks a small tributary drainage of Yeager Canyon. Because of the warm, south-facing exposure of this slope, this trail is most likely to remain free of snow and a good choice for winter hiking or riding. In summer, however, it is likely to be a very warm uphill hike.

At 0.7 miles the trail passes through a limestone outcropping. Also from this section of trail you can see Prescott Valley area and Glassford Hill (azimuth - 240 deg.) and Granite Dells (azimuth - 260 deg.). Just beyond this area you will come to a limestone point, an ideal spot for a rest or lunch break as you enjoy spectacular views to the west.

Along this section of trail you will note an abundance of pinyon pine trees. The pine cone crop during 1992 and 1993 was unusually abundant. When this occurs it is possible to collect several quarts of pine nuts in a short time by collecting cones and shaking the nuts from between the scales. Fall is the best time of year for collecting pinyon nuts.

At about 0.9 miles the trail becomes quite steep and the footing is slippery. The trail is on a more westerly exposure and provides a better view of the mountain peaks north of Highway 89A, especially Hickey Mountain at an elevation of 7,600 feet. To the right of this mountain you can see some of the inner basins of Mingus Mountain. The dramatic butte just north of the highway is a southeastern extension of Hickey Mountain, though almost 300 feet lower in elevation.

The trail drops rapidly through a series of switchbacks to the bottom of the small drainage that lies just south of Yeager Canyon. It then continues down this wash to its confluence with Yeager Canyon.

At 1.8 miles the trail intersects a road and then passes through an open gate. A fence lies across the right fork of this road. Continue left along the road to where the road crosses the creek on an old concrete bridge. Stay left here on this level trail as it wanders down through the attractive creek bottom.

At 2.3 miles the trail crosses the creek, a crossing that might be difficult during periods of high water. Just beyond this point you will come to the fiberglass trailhead sign.

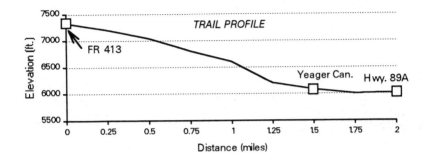

VIEW POINT TRAIL #106

General information:

This is one of several well-maintained trails serving the Mingus Mountain recreation area and campgrounds. The trails in this area and at these high elevations offer splendid views of the Verde Valley and the Cottonwood area to the east . In the fall this area is especially attractive when the maples and oaks turn to varying shades of red and brown, most notably the northern and western slopes of Mingus Mountain.

The trails in this area offer opportunities for several loop trips back to the campground area. Descending on Trail #106, the hiker can return to the campground by way of Trail #105A and Trail #105.

Access and trailhead location: Map: p. 102

If you are traveling either east from Prescott or west from Jerome on Highway 89A, take Forest Road 104 at the summit north of Mingus Mountain. Go south for approximately 2.6 miles to the Mingus Mountain campground. The trailhead is in the campground.

Road condition: The dirt road (FR 104) to the campground from Hwy. 89A is suitable for all vehicles if it is dry and free of snow. If you plan to visit the campground area in early spring, check with the Verde Valley District office at (602) 567-4121 to make sure that the road to the campground past the turnoff to FR 413 is open. The road to the campground beyond this point remains snow-covered and muddy much longer than the approach road from Hwy 89A. Its opening may be delayed well into May.

Hiking time: 1.5 hours to FR 413.   *Length:* 2.9 miles

Difficulty: Difficult, because of loose rock and steep slope.

Use: Moderate

Uses permitted: Hiking and horseback riding only.

Recommended seasons of use: spring, summer, fall

Maps, other resources: Prescott National Forest, east half; U.S.G.S. topographic 7.5′ quad for Cottonwood

Trail description:

Carry adequate water as there is none on this trail.

The trailhead is on the east edge of the campground. About 20 yards from the trailhead there is an overlook to the east where you will gain magnificent views of the Verde Valley and the Mogollon Rim.

Once you leave the rim the trail descends steeply and the vegetative cover changes quickly from a pine overstory to typical chaparral. This portion of the trail is quite steep, rocky, and badly eroded, and, consequently, is not suitable for horseback riding by inexperienced riders. Be particularly watchful of your footing here because of the loose rock and the possible presence of rattlesnakes.

At about 0.7 miles the trail heads in a northeasterly direction and the descent is more gradual. At 1.8 miles you will reach the junction with Trail #105A, a connector to Trail #105. The latter trail ascends the north side of Mingus Mtn. At this point you can either go northwest on Trail #105A and return to the campground area via Trail #105; or continue east for another 1.1 miles on Trail #106 to Allen Springs Road (FR 413).

Trail #105A is a very pleasant, shaded 0.5 mile walk in a northwesterly direction to where it intersects Trail #105. There are also some fine views along here of the Verde Valley.

Should you choose to continue on Trail #106 to FR 413, you will be traveling east on a steep, rocky descent for about the first 0.25 miles. The trail then contours more gradually around the north side of a ridge. Here the trail is shaded among pinyon pines. In the fall this would be a good area for collecting pinyon nuts. Within about 0.5 miles of leaving the junction with Trail #105A you will see that this trail begins to parallel Allen Springs Road. Shortly before reaching this road, it joins an old roadbed, and then within another 0.25 miles reaches the Allen Springs Road. The trailhead on this end is signed, and there is a good parking pull-off.

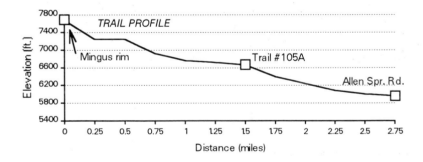

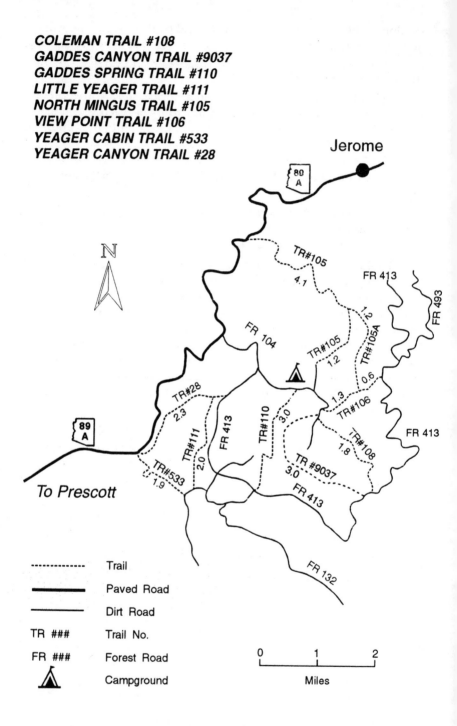

COLEMAN TRAIL #108
GADDES CANYON TRAIL #9037
GADDES SPRING TRAIL #110
LITTLE YEAGER TRAIL #111
NORTH MINGUS TRAIL #105
VIEW POINT TRAIL #106
YEAGER CABIN TRAIL #533
YEAGER CANYON TRAIL #28

Jerome

To Prescott

------------- Trail

Paved Road

Dirt Road

TR ### Trail No.

FR ### Forest Road

Campground

0   1   2

Miles

MARTIN CANYON TRAIL #103
RICK TANK CUTOFF #104

General information:

This trail runs along the southern border of the Woodchute Wilderness but does not enter the wilderness. Consequently, there are no restrictions as to type of travel permitted. It was originally built many years ago with a bulldozer and served as access to the cattle water tanks in Martin Canyon. These include Rich, Martin Canyon, Turkey, and Hickey Tanks. This old road now is part of the Prescott National Forest's trail network.

I would have to count this trail as one of my favorites, despite the difficulty of road access to it. Its charm lies in the fact that the trail follows Martin Canyon. Although the canyon does not have a perennial stream, subsurface water is sufficient to support a lush riparian vegetation of cottonwoods, boxelders, and Arizona walnuts. Although not obligated to riparian sites, Gambel oaks provide much of the remaining vegetative cover in this canyon. We hiked the canyon in the fall of 1993 and were rewarded with the delicious sights and smells of fall in the Arizona mountains. The deciduous trees provided colors yellow to ochre to dark brown. In addition the fallen leaves and pine needles padded much of the trail for a quiet, soft walk.

Since one must walk the canyon bottom itself, I would recommend this trail for the dry fall of the year. During spring this canyon probably carries a heavy runoff from Woodchute Mountain and hiking it would require walking in water much of the way.

Access and trailhead location: Map: p. 108

To reach the east end of the trail, travel north from downtown Prescott on Highway 89 then east on Highway 89A for a total distance of about 25 miles. At the Mingus road summit turn left (north) to the Potato Patch Campground. Take the campground entrance road. Within a quarter-mile a paved road turns left. Take this road to the graveled parking area. Take the gravel road that leaves this area through a green-painted gate. Within a short distance this road becomes suitable only for high-clearance vehicles. Continue along this rough road past a power substation (0.3 miles from parking), then past the fenced wildlife water area to the trailhead sign for Trail #102 (0.7 miles). Then turn west from here past Hickey Tank (1.3 miles). At miles 1.7 the road forks; stay right. At 1.9 miles this rough road turn sharply downhill along a very rocky grade. Do not go beyond this point unless equipped with 4WD. You will pass a water tank on the left (not visible from road) before descending to Turkey Tank to the right of the road. You will recognize this pond from the remains of a deer hunting platform in a tree just above the pond. Park here. The total distance from the Potato Patch parking area is 2.8 miles.

Road condition: FR 106, though rough, is suitable for high clearance vehicles. The road off the canyon rim to Turkey Tank is only suitable for 4WD vehicle.

Hiking time: 3.5 hours round-trip.   *Length:* 4.5 miles to end of canyon.

Difficulty: Easy.   *Use:* Light.

Uses permitted: Motorized uses permitted, though portions of trail are impassable to even 4WD vehicles.

Recommended seasons of use: spring, summer, fall

Maps, other resources: Prescott National Forest, east half; U.S.G.S. topographic 7.5' quad for Hickey Mountain.

Trail description:

Unless you plan to negotiate more of this trail by vehicle, Turkey Tank is a logical starting point for a hike. Driving beyond here along this kidney-busting route would remove much of the pleasure of the place.

At 0.4 miles the road enters the main part of Martin Canyon. The rocks of the roadbed here are so tightly placed that the road resembles a cobblestone street, though rougher to be sure. Where the trail is not in the wash itself, it is well-padded with pine needles and oak leaves, thus providing a quiet, comfortable walking surface.

At 1.5 miles the trail surface within the drainage becomes increasingly difficult to walk on, not to mention drive. It is in this area that the trail is virtually impassable to vehicles.

As the canyon descends to mile 1.8, it begins to broaden considerably. The south-facing slopes are now covered with brush and scattered alligator juniper. At mile 2.2 you will reach Rick Tank. A short trail goes to the tank while the main trail turns sharply to the right, entering the canyon bottom.

At 2.9 miles a very large juniper tree with a girth of 17 feet stands on the north bank of the wash. The roadbed in this vicinity showed some recent use and appears to be more drivable than the upper end. This portion of the road is probably reached from Lonesome Valley rather than the rim of the canyon. We did not search out an access route from this direction, although maps indicate that remote ranch roads provide a route to the western extremity of the trail where it exits Martin Canyon near James Tank.

We ended our exploration of the trail at mile 3.3 about a mile from where it leaves the canyon. We do not recommend this trail for a one-way trip with vehicles at both ends. The road access to the western end from Hwy. 89A involves a 14-mile round-trip over rough roads. Also, the trail is short enough that a return along the same route to the Martin Canyon Tank starting point takes less than 4 hours.

Tip!

Here's a suggestion for a longer, round-trip hike or ride. Drive to the trailhead for the Woodchute Trail #102. Park here. Walk the 2.8 miles of road to Martin Canyon. Then go another 2.2 miles to Rick Tank as described above. Another trail (#104) goes almost due east from Rick Tank to Woodchute Tank adjacent to the Woodchute Trail, a distance of 1.1 miles. Trail #104 to Woodchute Tank is within the Woodchute Wilderness and the only uses permitted are hiking and horseback riding. Then hike or ride an additional 2.4 miles south on the Woodchute Trail to your parked car. The total distance for this hike would be about 8.3 miles, just slightly longer than a two-way trip into Martin Canyon and back.

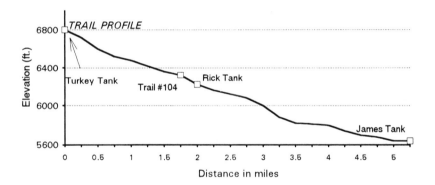

WOODCHUTE TRAIL #102

General information:

This trail bisects the Woodchute Wilderness, a 5,700-acre area designated as wilderness by Congress in 1984. The portion of the wilderness trail on the south side of Woodchute Mountain was established along what was once a bulldozer track. The bulldozer was used to create several cattle watering tanks on Woodchute Mountain. An open stand of second growth Ponderosa pine covers the mountain top, the original forest having been completely cut years ago. When the copper mines at Jerome were in operation, loggers obtained shoring timbers for the mines from this mountain. They transported the logs by way of a chute extending down the north side of the mountain to loading platforms for the narrow gauge railroad which served Jerome. That railroad track is now FR 318. There are splendid panoramic views from the mountaintop in all directions. The view to the northeast, however, is especially spectacular. From the rim of the mountain you gain a view of the entire Verde Valley, Sycamore Canyon, and the Flagstaff area mountain peaks — San Francisco Peaks, Bill Williams Mtn., and the several volcanic peaks in between.

Access and trailhead location: Map: p. 108

The best access to this trail is from Hwy. 89A. Go to the Potato Patch Campground just east of the summit on 89A. A paved entrance to the campground leaves Hwy. 89A just opposite FR 104 which goes to the Methodist Camp and the Mingus Campground. Take the campground entrance road. Within a quarter-mile a paved road turns left. Take this road to the graveled parking area. Take the gravel road that leaves this area through a green-painted gate. Within a short distance this road becomes suitable only for high-clearance vehicles. Continue along this rough road past a power substation, then past the fenced wildlife water area to the trailhead sign for Trail #102. The total distance on this road from the graveled parking area is about 0.6 miles.

You can also reach the north trailhead from the Chino Valley area by way of FR 354. Take this road to just south of Perkinsville. Then take FR 318 south from there, then west on FR 318A for 1.3 miles to the north trailhead. Access from Jerome is also by way of FR 318 that goes around the north side of Woodchute Mountain.

Road condition: Paved to the southern access. The dirt roads to the northern access are suitable for high clearance vehicles.

Hiking time: 2.5 hours to Woodchute suumit.

Length: 7.4 miles from Potato Patch campground to north trailhead on FR 318A; 4.5 miles to rim viewpoint; 3.75 miles to Woodchute Mtn. summit.

Difficulty: Moderate if going only to summit, difficult if traveling entire length.

Use: Moderate.

Uses permitted: Hiking and horseback riding only.

Recommended seasons of use: spring, summer, fall

Maps, other resources: Prescott National Forest, east half; U.S.G.S. topographic 7.5′ quads for Hickey Mountain and Munds Draw.

Trail description:

From the south trailhead it is a steady, easy climb of 3.75 miles through open stands of second-growth ponderosa pine to the top of Woodchute Mountain. As you reach the summit the trail becomes more shaded as you travel under a closed forest canopy. It is then another 0.75 miles to the north rim of the mountain to where you can obtain the best views to the north and east. You will need to leave the trail, going east for a short distance to reach the most spectacular viewpoints. This is a good place at which to stop if you plan to return to the Potato Patch campground.

Should you choose to continue down the north side to the north trailhead, it is another 2.9 miles to FR 318A. This road then goes northeast for about 1.3 miles to where it connects to the old narrow gauge road (FR 318) to Jerome. The south ascent is the easiest and most popular route since it only climbs 600 feet to the summit. From the top at 7,700 ft. to the north trailhead, however, the descent is 2,260 feet. There are some steep switchbacks on this side.

Caution: There is no drinking water along this trail, so carry sufficient water for the round-trip.

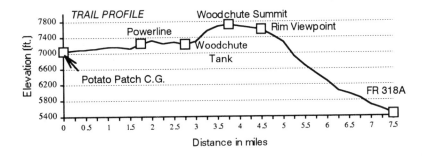

MARTIN CANYON TRAIL #103
RICK TANK CUTOFF #104
WOODCHUTE TRAIL #102

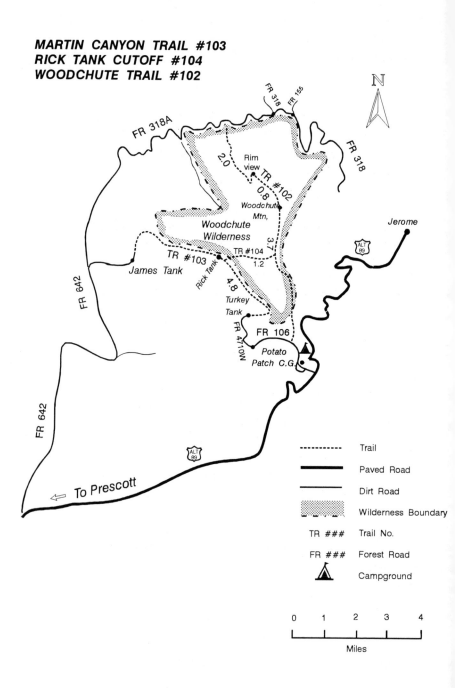

        MINGUS MOUNTAIN

Sierra Prieta

THIS RING OF LOW PINE-COVERED MOUNTAINS forms the southwestern rim of the high basin that includes the city of Prescott. The name derives from the Spanish meaning "dark mountain." Similarly Lt. A. W. Whipple in his 1853 journals referred to these mountains as "Black Mesa," because they were dark or black with juniper trees.

During the years immediately following the Gadsden Purchase, it was gold that attracted many to the remote Arizona Territory and the mountains around Prescott. Indeed, there seems not an acre within this region of hills that doesn't contain at least an exploratory dig.

Much like the Bradshaw Mountains, this area is underlain with mostly intrusive rock — granites, quartz, and metamorphic schists. Thumb Butte, though treated as a separate section with respect to its trails, is actually part of this range. It is an exception in its geologic origin in that the butte is very dark extrusive basalt. An example of a surface quartz vein occurs on the Sierra Prieta Trail described in this section.

The highest elevations along the crest of the Sierra Prietas are cool and wet enough to support a mixed conifer vegetation type of ponderosa pine, white fir, and Douglas fir. At lower elevations the vegetation gradually changes to more xeric types — evergreen oaks, pinyon pines, alligator juniper. Finally, at even lower elevations dense almost impenetrable stands of brush predominate.

A diverse flora also produces a diverse spectrum of wildlife — from elk, bears, deer, javelina, and mountain lions to Aberts squirrels, Merriams turkeys, and a host of mountain dwelling song birds and raptors.

The major drainages from this small mountain range, in contrast to the Bradshaws, flow north ultimately into the Verde River system. Most of these stream channels converge on the city of Prescott. It is the riparian vegetation of these stream courses that provides Prescott with dramatic fall color, but also the delicate yellow-greens of spring that contrast so noticeably with the dark conifer forest backdrop.

ASPEN CREEK TRAIL #48

General information:
This is a scenic trail offering wonderful views of the western slope of the Bradshaw Mountains, Peeples Valley, and northward to Bill Williams Mtn. and the San Francisco Peaks. Since the trail has a gradient of over 1,600 feet, it passes through a range of vegetation types from brush and cactus covered hills at its southern extremity to tall pines and deciduous oaks near Aspen Creek. The trail passes through some areas treated about 10 years ago with herbicides to improve grass production. Since then the area appears to have been increasingly attractive to deer and even elk. Although not often seen, elk sign is much in evidence.

Access and trailhead location: Map: p. 116
Because of the large elevational change, we recommend hiking this trail from north to south. To access the north trailhead, take Montezuma St. (Hwy. 89) in Prescott from its junction with Gurley St. south for 1.1 miles to the junction with Copper Basin Rd.; turn right on Copper Basin Rd. and continue for 4.7 miles. The trailhead will be on the left of the road just 0.2 miles past where the road crosses Aspen Creek.

Road condition: Paved, then graded dirt on Copper Basin Road.

Hiking time: 4 hours.   *Length:* 5.5 miles

Difficulty: Difficult in places because of poor footing.

Use: Light

Uses permitted: Hiking, horseback riding, bicycling (non-motorized).

Recommended seasons of use: Spring, fall, winter; lower elevations could be quite warm in summer.

Maps, other resources: Prescott National Forest, west half; U.S.G.S. topographic 7.5' quads for Prescott, Iron Springs, and Wilhoit.

Trail description:
The trail actually begins on FR 9415, marked by a vertical fiberglass sign. This primitive road climbs steeply for 0.2 miles around the northwest side of the hill overlooking Aspen Creek. At 0.2 miles the road turn east and levels out considerably. In this area the road passes through a nice open stand of ponderosa pines, Gambel oaks, and alligator junipers. At 0.4 miles, look due north for a splendid view of Bill Williams Mtn. and the San Francisco Peaks.

At 0.5 miles Thumb Butte comes into view on left. Be on the lookout for a 4 inch square post on the right next to a large Gambel oak tree. The trail at this point turns sharply to the right. You soon get a wonderful view of the west side of the northern end of the Bradshaw mountains and its most prominent peaks — Spruce Mtn., Mt.Union, Mt. Tritle, and Maverick Mtn. This is a well maintained section of trail, with numerous erosion control logs placed across the trail.

At 0.8 miles the trail descends into a small wash and a stand of large Gambel oaks. The trail crosses this wash and climbs steeply into pine forest. There is much evidence of tassel-eared (Aberts) squirrel activity here. They feed on the inner bark layers of twigs and in so doing clip the terminal cluster of needles that then fall to the ground.

At 1.5 miles the trail reaches a ridge marked by a large juniper on the right. At 1.7 miles the trail leaves the cooler north slope descending into a mix of brush species, pinyon pine, and alligator juniper.

At 1.9 miles the trail reaches another small ridge and a wonderful view of the southern Bradshaws. Just a bit farther there is another view to the south of the southern Bradshaws. If you look just to the right of Maverick Mt. you will see on the far horizon the fire lookout tower atop Towers Mtn.

At 2.2 miles you begin to get the first look at Mt. Francis on your right. This mountain top is the site of TV translators and other electronic equipment that brings both antenna and cable television to the Prescott area. In this section of trail you will pass through an area of stark, bleached out remains of Emory and white oaks. Some of this area was treated some 10 years ago with herbicides to improve grass production.

At 2.8 miles pay close attention to the direction the trail is taking. The trail after coming up the drainage, takes a sharp turn to the right. It then crosses a ridge where you gain a view of a large drainage to the west.

At 3.0 miles there is a routed-wood trail sign at a T-intersection. The sign indicates that the left fork goes to Copper Creek (1.5 miles; actually closer to 2.5 miles), the right fork to Mt. Francis (1 mile). The route to the right also provides access to Copper Basin Rd., a distance of 1.5 miles.

Tassel-eared Squirrel

At 3.3 miles and traveling along a southbound ridge, one has the best views of two worlds. Looking east you can now see the entire west-facing slope of the Bradshaw Mountains. If you are unfamiliar with the Bradshaw Mountain peaks and happen to be carrying a compass, here are some azimuths to some of the major landscape features: Spruce Mtn.- 100 deg., Mt. Union - 140 deg., Maverick Mtn. - 148 deg., Towers Mtn. - 152, Peeples Valley - 125. These azimuths also assume that you have preset a declination constant of 14 deg. on the compass.

At mile 3.7 the trail descends steeply through a series of sharp switchbacks towards the Copper Creek drainage. It soon reaches a T-intersection with the East Copper Trail #260 which goes northwest and southeast from here. Trail #260 permits the use of motorcycles although Trail #48 does not. Take the left fork here to reach the Copper Creek road and Highway 89.

Going in a generally southeasterly direction, the trail has left pine forest far behind and enters lower elevations where brush and evergreen oaks predominate. At 4.1 miles you will come to a 3-wire fence and then a wire gate. Do not be tempted to go through the gate to the left; the trail continues straight. At 4.5 miles and all along this section of the trail the surface is extremely rocky and the footing very unstable.

At 4.8 miles the trail narrows considerably and the footing remains tricky. Here the trail joins an old 4-wheel drive road. Continue to the right at this junction for about 25 yards. The trail then turns left away from the road near a large pile of rocks to warn of this turn.

At 5.1 miles you will come to an old mining road and then a mine tailings pile on the right. About 50 feet from the mine tailings the trail switches back to the left; do not be tempted to follow the road to the right. At mile 5.3 the trail is quite steep and the surface very loose; be extremely careful of your footing in this area.

At 5.7 miles the trail intersects Copper Creek Rd. (FR 53). Take this road south for 0.4 miles to Hwy. 89.

Tip! Park one vehicle on Copper Creek Rd. (FR 53) at the trail intersection and a second vehicle at the trailhead on Aspen Creek to allow a one-way downhill hike to the south. The one-way trip by paved road from one end of the trail to the other takes approximately 30 minutes, a distance of 9.5 miles.

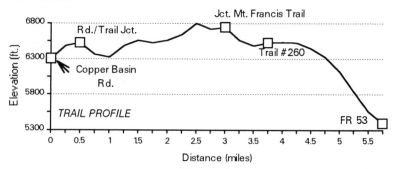

WEST SPRUCE TRAIL #264

General information:

The trail is suitable for day hikes or rides in the area. It offers some magnificent high elevation vistas of much of northern Arizona, from Skull Valley on the west to Mingus Mountain on the east. The Sierra Prieta range was heavily mined during the early part of this century. There are ample opportunities to explore the remains of some of this mining exploration. On the approach to West Spruce Mtn. you enter a mixed conifer vegetation type with an abundance of uneven-aged Douglas fir, Gambel oak, and pine. Do not waste your time looking for spruce; there are none here despite the name of the mountain. The southern exposures will be mostly pinyon pine, juniper, and evergreen oaks grading into brush species of the chaparral vegetation type at the lower elevations.

If you take a side trail over to Williams Peak during summer, you are likely to encounter an unusual natural phenomenon: swarms of ladybugs (more correctly ladybeetles) blanket trees, bushes, and rocks in concentrations exceeding 120 million per acre on the higher peaks of the Bradshaws and Sierra Prietas. Although they can be gathered by the quart, don't bother taking them home. The ladybugs at this time of year are in a period of estivation (dormancy), neither feeding nor mating, and will not feed on your garden insects.

Access and trailhead location: Map: p. 116

This trail is divided into two sections. To reach the south end of the northern section, take Iron Springs Road west from the intersection of Iron Springs, Willow Creek, Whipple, and Miller Valley roads in Prescott for 7.0 miles to the turnoff to the Highland Pines residential area (Skyline Drive). Follow Skyline Drive through the residential area to the end of the subdivision for a total distance of 2.9 miles from Iron Springs Rd. A dirt road continues south (FR 47) for 0.5 miles to a large highway type sign showing the road to the trailhead. Take the 4WD road to the right. The trailhead sign is about 0.4 miles farther.

A 1.3 miles section of FR 47B actually links the south end of one section of Trail #264 to the north end of the other section of Trail #264. To reach the northern end of the northern section, take Iron Springs Road from the 4-way intersection for about 8.1 miles. Then turn left onto the Dosie Pit road and go for 2.7 miles to the well-marked trailhead on the left of the road.

You can reach the southern section of Trail #264 by way of FR 373, just north of the Sierra Prieta Overlook. From Prescott take Gurley St. west for approximately 2 miles to Thumb Butte Road. Continue on

Thumb Butte Road to the Thumb Butte recreation area. Then at 1.0 miles past the picnic area stay left at the turn to Aloma Camp. Then, 0.6 miles past this junction, turn left on FR 373. From here travel south on FR 373 for 3.3 miles. The trailhead sign will be on the right of the road just as you reach the ridge top. This point is approximately 0.5 miles north of the Sierra Prieta Overlook.

Road condition: The access road from Highland Pines is suitable for high clearance vehicle as far as the large trail sign. From there the road is only suitable for 4-wheel drive vehicles. The northern access along Dosie Pit Road (old railroad grade) is dirt but suitable for all vehicles if the weather is good.

Hiking time: 5 hours for the entire trail.   *Length:* 7.4 miles

Difficulty: Moderate   *Use:* Moderate

Uses permitted: Hiking, horseback riding, bicycling (non-motorized)

Recommended seasons of use: Spring, fall, winter.

Maps, other resources: Prescott National Forest, west half; U.S.G.S. topographic 7.5' quad for Iron Springs.

Trail description:

From just north of the Sierra Prieta overlook the trail travels northwest just across a drainage from Williams Peak, staying close to the top of the ridge. You will encounter some enormous old alligator junipers within the first half mile. At mile 0.5 there is a wonderful panorama to the west of Skull Valley and the mountains beyond. The trail then stays in open stands of pine and Gambel oak and an understory of ceanothus (buck brush). At mile 0.6, there is a grand view to the northeast of Granite Mountain, Bill Williams Mountain, and nearby Williams Peak. A short side trail (unmarked) at the rail fence next to a massive alligator juniper (mile 0.65) heads over to Williams Peak.

The main trail continues along or close to the crest of the Sierra Prieta. At mile 1.8 there is a wire gate on the left.

At mile 1.9 you will encounter an old road blocked to access by a short rail fence; stay to the left.

At mile 3.0 you will start to see some Douglas Fir trees and an abundance of clipped twigs of ponderosa pine. Tassel-eared (Aberts) squirrels produce these clippings as they feed on the soft inner bark of twigs. As they bite off the ends of selected branches, the terminal portion with its cluster of pine needles, falls to the ground.

At mile 3.7, after climbing a set of switchbacks to a ridge, you will encounter an old routed-wood sign. It shows the mileage southeast to Copper Basin and Thumb Butte Rd. and the distance (0.25 miles) northwest to West Spruce Mountain. There is also a trail opposite this sign that goes almost due north down the drainage just to the west of Porter Mountain. This trail connects with FR 47 and the Highland Pines residential area (1.5 miles).

Take the trail to West Spruce Mountain if you wish to continue on Trail #264. In just 0.7 miles the trail will join FR 47B. The direction to the right goes to Highland Pines. If you continue left along FR 47B for another 1.3 miles, you will encounter the other end of Trail #264 coming in from the north at Sugarloaf Mountain. The trail then begins a long twisting descent to Iron Springs wash. The trail enters the wash in an attractive stand of netleaf hackberry trees. In the dry November of 1992 there was a live stream there, so I suspect that this wash may have water much of the year. This water, however, is likely to be polluted from cattle use.

The trail then proceeds upstream for 100 yards to the 4" x 4" post on the north side of the wash. The well-maintained trail from here west to FR 9271A takes you through very dense stands of chaparral and pinyon pine. The pines in the fall of 1992 were heavy with cones and a good yield of edible seeds. In developing the profile of this trail, we have not included the road that connects from the Highland Pines area.

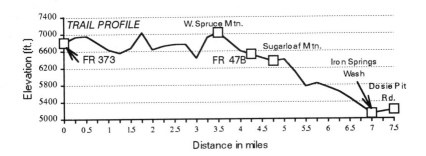

ASPEN CREEK TRAIL #48
WEST SPRUCE TRAIL #264

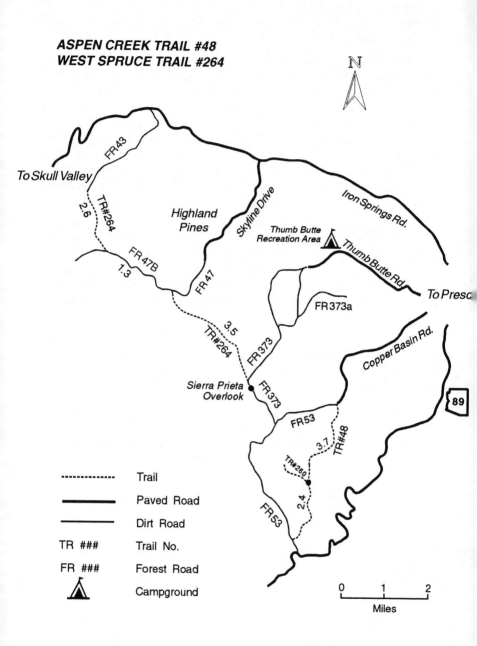

N

To Skull Valley

FR43

TR#264
2.6

FR 47B
1.3

Highland
Pines

Skyline Drive

FR47

TR#264
3.5

FR373

Sierra Prieta
Overlook

FR373

Iron Springs Rd.

Thumb Butte
Recreation Area

Thumb Butte Rd.

To Presc

FR373a

Copper Basin Rd.

89

FR53

TR#260
TR#48
3.7

2.4

FR53

To Presc

-------------- Trail

—————— Paved Road

—————— Dirt Road

TR ### Trail No.

FR ### Forest Road

⛺ Campground

0   1   2

Miles

SIERRA PRIETA TRAIL

This trail is another in the series of trails traversing the crest of the Sierra Prietas. Typical of the trails along this crest, it offers some dramatic views in all directions. On clear dry days, one can see in awesome solitary splendor the snow-covered flanks of the San Francisco Peaks, the highest of which is Mt. Humphreys, almost 13,000 feet in elevation.

Close to the city of Prescott, the trail offers a modest day hike for city residents and visitors. It also provides some great views of the city and the surrounding hills.

Switching frequently from northerly to more southerly exposures, the trail also provides a look at greatly varying vegetation types from almost pure stands of ponderosa pine to treeless brushlands of evergreen shrubs, agave, yuccas, and cacti.

Access and Trailhead Location   Map: p. 120

I will describe this trail from west to east beginning where it connects with the northern terminus of Aspen Creek Trail #48. To reach Trail #48, drive south on Montezuma St. (Hwy. 89) in downtown Prescott south for 1.1 miles to the junction with Copper Basin Rd. Turn right on Copper Basin Rd. and continue for 4.7 miles. The trailhead will be on the left of the road just 0.2 miles past where the road crosses Aspen Creek.

Road condition: Paved along Copper Basin Rd. for about 2 miles, then dirt; suitable for all vehicles

Hiking time: 3.5 hrs.   *Length:* 4.6 miles

Difficulty: Moderate

Use: Heavy between Quartz Mtn. and Hwy. 89

Recommended seasons of use: Spring, fall, winter

Maps, other resources: Prescott National Forest map, west half; U.S.G.S. topographic 7.5' quads for Iron Springs, Prescott, and Wilhoit.

Trail Description

Trail #48 actually begins on FR 9415, marked by a vertical fiberglass sign. This marker shows the permissible uses of the trail to be hiking, horseback riding, and bicycling. There is also a decal indicating that motorcycles are permitted, but this decal is almost completely scraped off. This primitive road climbs steeply for 0.2 miles around the northwest side of the hill overlooking Aspen Creek. At 0.2 miles the road turn east and levels out considerably. The road surface was snow and ice covered when we hiked it in January 1993. In this area the road passes through a nice open stand of ponderosa pines, Gambel oaks, and alligator junipers. At 0.4 miles, look due north for a splendid view of Bill Williams Mtn. and the San Francisco Peaks.

At 0.5 miles Thumb Butte comes into view on left. Be on the lookout for a 4-inch square post on the right next to a large Gambel oak tree. At one time this post probably held a trail sign. At this point Trail #48 turns sharply to the right toward Mt. Francis. Our trail goes east following the 4-wheel drive road (FR 9415). At 0.9 miles this road forks; take the left fork.

At mile 1.1 the road, quite rocky now, climbs steeply, then enters a nice open stand of ponderosa pine.

At mile 1.2 another primitive road turns sharply left, at almost a right angle to our direction of travel. This spur leads within a short distance to an overlook. Though screened by trees, one can see the southern edge of Thumb Butte.

At mile 1.3 there is a clearing and an open vista of the Sierra Prietas and Mt. Francis (azimuth 232 deg.). Just beyond this vista point the trail turns north.

At mile 1.7 there is an opening in the trees permitting a wonderful view of Mt. Union and to its right Mt. Tritle. Mt. Union (azimuth of 130 deg.) still covered with a heavy blanket of snow in early March. To its right on an azimuth of 150 deg. is Mt. Tritle. This latter peak is most visible from downtown Prescott and usually has a blanket of snow well into May.

Just beyond this point you will come to a heavy steel gate. Though this gate was open when we hiked, it is probably closed and locked at certain times. Just beyond the gate is a Forest Service trail sign (FR 9415) indicating that hiking, horseback riding, and bicycling are permitted. An additional decal below (probably a motorcycle) was obliterated, most likely by someone attempting to discourage motorized use on this trail. Take the trail to the right where it leaves the 4-wheel drive road.

At mile 1.9 the trail heads northeast and comes into an opening that offers a wonderful view of the northern Bradshaw Mountains, Goldwater Lake, and in the foreground, Quartz Mountain. This little hill is covered with roads that were apparently used for the transport of rock from the now abandoned quarry. The top of this hill and its exposed outcropping of white milky quartz, glistens in the sunlight.

The trail as it circles below the top of Wolverton Mountain is easy to follow though very narrow. Its surface is quite rocky and hikers need to be careful of their footing. Now on the eastern slope of Wolverton Mountain, vegetation is more open, composed of mountain mahogany,

118   *SIERRA PRIETA*

Emory oaks, scrub oaks, and a few scattered pines. The pockets of Gambel oak in the draws offer a shady rest in hot weather.

At mile 2.3 the trail, after descending a steep rough and rocky slope, comes out of the more open chaparral into a more closed canopy of pines, junipers, and Gambel oak as you approach Quartz Mtn.

The narrow portion of the trail ends at mile 2.6 in an opening, a circular road probably used as turnaround for large trucks carrying rock materials taken from Quartz Mtn. Another Forest Service sign (FR 9415) indicates that the only permissible uses of this roadway are hiking and horseback riding; the two lower decals have been obliterated. The ground here glistens with a fine coating of crushed quartz rock.

The short climb to the top of Quartz Mtn. rewards the climber with a splendid 360 deg. view of the surrounding country. The quartz outcropping here is worth noting because of its color. Besides the various veins of color running through the rock itself, the quartz is covered with a variegated coating of lichen varying in color from light yellow to green to a soft charcoal black.

Returning to the main road, take the lower of the two roads going around the southern end of Quartz Mtn. There is a loading chute just east of the road junction, but avoid this crumbling structure.

At mile 3.1. you will encounter a wire gate, and just beyond that the junction with the road coming around the north side of Quartz Mt.

At mile 3.9 the trail intersects a well-traveled dirt road. Follow this road east for 0.7 miles to its junction with Highway 89 near the Prescott Pines Mobile Home Resort.

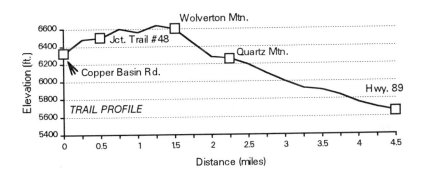

SIERRA PRIETA TRAIL

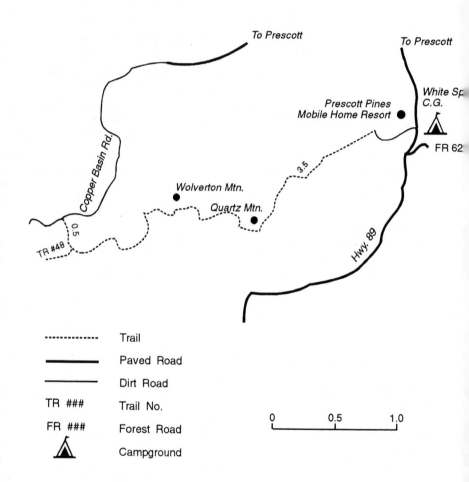

Trail

Paved Road

Dirt Road

TR ###   Trail No.

FR ###   Forest Road

Campground

| 0 | 0.5 | 1.0 |

Thumb Butte Area

THIS DARK BASALT ROCK SITS BARELY 1,000 FEET ABOVE THE SURROUNDING LANDSCAPE. Nonetheless, its isolation from other ridges and peaks gives it prominence. This is obvious if you look at the number of local businesses that use that butte profile as an element of their business logo.

This butte lies at the western edge of the city of Prescott and, consequently, receives heavy use. The Forest Service recreation area at the base of the butte features 20 picnic tables and 2 picnic areas that can be reserved for use by groups. There are no camping sites.

Hiking trails near Thumb Butte form a confusing network. Many of these extend from residential developments across other private properties to connect with public land trails. Hikers and horseback riders have been using these "unofficial" trails for many years. However, because residential development has been leapfrogging farther into forested areas, many trail users are finding themselves cut off from traditional pathways. The Yavapai Trails Association, an umbrella group representing trail users, has been attempting to negotiate public access rights for non-motorized use of some of these traditional trails. Even where legal public access is lacking, property owners when asked are often willing to allow hikers to cross their land. However, the proliferation of all-terrain vehicles and motorcycles and their use on public and private lands is causing vegetation destruction, erosion of trails, and noise pollution. This only gives private property owners more reasons for building fences and locking gates.

Some trails described in this section begin or end on private property. A little courtesy and respect for the landowners' rights will go a long ways toward ensuring continued access to your favorite wild places.

LONG'S CANYON TRAIL #316

General information:

In the database of Forest Service trails information, this trail is named the "Pine Lakes Trail." The trail, however, does not go to Pine Lakes. Consequently, I have taken the liberty of using a trail name that appears on some hand-drawn local maps of the area.

It is close enough to Pine Lakes and other residential and recreational developments on Prescott's west side to provide a pleasant and short canyon hike. Also, since it connects with many other private and public land trails, one can work out a complex of hiking or riding recipes (routes) to suit almost any taste.

Access and trailhead location: Map: p. 132

To reach the south end of Trail #316, drive west from downtown Prescott on Gurley Street for 2.5 miles to Thumb Butte Road. Continue northwest on Thumb Butte Road for 1.5 miles to the Thumb Butte recreation site and the picnic area. The trailhead for Trail #316 is just about 25 yards north of the three stone steps at picnic table #8.

To reach the north end of the trail, travel north from downtown Prescott on Montezuma Street for 1.75 miles to the 4-way intersection. Continue west on Iron Springs Road from this junction for another 2.6 miles to Hereford Road, which is just opposite the turnoff to the Wildwood Estates. Go south on Hereford Road for a short distance to the Kingswood tennis courts. Turn left here, and then within a few yards, left again, leaving the paved road and traveling east on the gravel road of the old railroad grade. This road lies astride a portion of the rail line that once connected Prescott with the rail junction at Seligman. Travel about 0.4 miles on this dirt road. Just before reaching Camp Yavapines, there is a concrete bunker below and just to the south of the road. An obscure trail leaves to the south of the road about 100 yards west of this spot. It climbs a short but steep hill, crosses a flattened barbed-wire fence and intersects another trail going east and west. The west leg connects to Trail #316.

Road condition: Paved.   *Hiking time:* 1 hour.

Length: 1.2 miles to Prescott National Forest boundary; 1.7 miles to old railroad grade road.

Difficulty: Easy.   *Use:* Moderate.

Uses permitted: Hiking, horseback riding, and bicycling (non-motorized).

Recommended seasons of use: All seasons.

Maps, other resources: Prescott National Forest, west half; U.S.G.S. topographic 7.5' quad for Iron Springs.

Trail description:

The trail starts at the northwest end of the Thumb Butte picnic area just north of Table #8. It travels almost due north from this point, passing through a gate at 0.1 miles. Since this portion of the trail ascends a south-facing slope, the surrounding country is quite open and sunny. Scrub oaks, manzanita, and pinyon pines dominate the landscape. Consequently, a hike started late on a summer day can be very warm indeed.

At mile 0.3 there is a well-marked junction with Trail #317, which goes west from here. Then just a few yards north of this junction, the eastern leg of Trail #317 heads east to the National Forest boundary. It connects through private land to the Forest Trails residential community. After passing these two junctions, Trail #316 begins a steep descent down a brush-covered rocky ravine. By the 0.8-mile point, however, it becomes much more shaded and pine needles cushion the trail.

At mile 1.2 an aluminum gate marks the National Forest boundary. A trail through private land continues to parallel the wash for another 0.5 miles to the old railroad grade road. Just before reaching this road, a branch of this trail goes east and ends within the Camp Yavapines property.

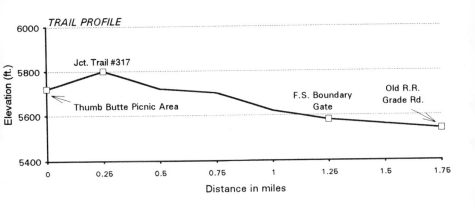

RIDGE TRAIL #317

General information:

This trail, when combined with the southern end of Trail #316, makes a loop route that begins and ends at the Thumb Butte Picnic Area. It goes through a diverse forest of ponderosa pine, pinyon pine, alligator juniper, and chaparral brush species, depending on the direction in which the trail slope is facing. There are some unobstructed views of the western end of the Sierra Prietas, the Highland Pines residential area, and Granite Mountain. At the eastern extremity of the trail you get a different and dramatic view of the northwest face of Thumb Butte and the Prescott area. This is a fairly level, well-shaded trail that provides a very pleasant one to two hour hike. It is also an excellent route for mountain biking.

Access and trailhead location: Map: p. 132

The middle section of Trail #317 is reached from Trail #316. Travel west on Gurley Street from downtown Prescott for 2.5 miles to Thumb Butte Rd. Continue northwest on Thumb Butte Rd. for 1.5 miles to the recreation site. The trailhead for Trail #316 is just about 25 yards north of the three stone steps at picnic table #8.

I recommend that you hike or ride this trail from west to east, ending your trip at the Thumb Butte Picnic Area or continuing east to the Forest boundary. There is an alternative to reaching Trail #317 via the picnic area. Leave your vehicle at the Thumb Butte Picnic Area and walk or ride west on Thumb Butte Road for one more mile. Turn right on the first dirt road that you encounter. Go just 0.25 miles to the top of the hill but no farther. The trail heads both east and west from here directly away from this parking area, although there are no trail signs. The west leg of the trail goes for about 0.5 miles before intersecting with the dirt road to the Willow Springs Girl Scout Camp. I will describe the portion of this trail that goes east.

To reach Trail #317 from the Forest Trails residential area, drive north from downtown Prescott on Montezuma Street for 1.75 miles to the 4-way intersection. Continue west on Iron Springs Road for another 1.75 miles to the Forest Trails sign on the left of the road. Turn south here on Sierry Peaks Road and go for about 1 mile. The access trail to Trail #317 is atop a rust-red rocky bluff about 100 yards west of the green-painted water tower and 0.4 miles north of road Forest View North. This is private property and because of recent development there you might need to get local permission to access the trail from this point.

Road condition: Paved to the Thumb Butte Picnic Area.

Hiking time: 1.5 hours

Length: 1.6 miles including Trail #316.

Difficulty: Easy.   ***Use:*** Moderate.

Uses permitted: Hiking, horseback riding, and bicycling.

Recommended season of use: spring, summer, fall

Maps, other resources: Prescott National Forest, west half; U.S.G.S. topographic 7.5' quad for Iron Springs.

Trail description:

From the western end, the trail climbs in an easterly direction along an abandoned, badly rutted road. It contours through shaded forest cover around the north side of a 6,000-foot hill. It is in this area that you discover some dramatic views to the northwest, particularly when the air is clear and swelling cumulus clouds fill the summer sky. To your left will be the Highland Pines residential area and the western end of the Sierra Prietas. To the north is the rocky crest of Granite Mountain.

At about the 1-mile point the vegetation is more open and shrubby, allowing some splendid views of Thumb Butte and the Prescott area. At mile 1.25 Trail #317 intersects with Trail #316.

Just a few yards north of this intersection, Trail #317 continues east. It climbs up a small knoll and then up a second hill, neither of which is steep. The trail then continues east, passing through a stand of sickly pinyon pines, devasted by scale disease. At 0.7 miles from the trail junction with Trail #316, it reaches the Forest Service boundary fence and gate. Another trail continues east from here through private property to the Forest Trails residential community.

If you wish to finish your trip at the Thumb Butte Picnic Area, take Trail #316 south from the junction with Trail #317.

A caution: Be careful of where you place your hands and your feet. The presence of rattlesnakes is always a possibility in warm weather. On our last trip on this trail, we encountered an Arizona blacktail rattlesnake, well-hidden in the shade of a rock ledge. We left it just as we found it.

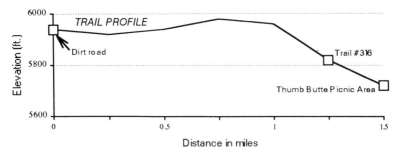

TRAIL PROFILE

Dirt road

Trail #316

Thumb Butte Picnic Area

THUMB BUTTE TRAIL #33

General information:

Because of its proximity to the city of Prescott, this is one of the most popular and heavily used trails on the Prescott National Forest. There are signs along the trail identifying individual plants and vegetation types. Directional signs are well maintained and helpful. This is a well-maintained trail having rest areas, water bars to control erosion, and a wide right-of-way. The ridge just below the basaltic crest of Thumb Butte offers excellent panoramic views of the Prescott area, the Bradshaw Mountains, Sierra Prietas, Granite Mountain, Mingus Mountain, and, on a clear day, the San Francisco Peaks.

Access and trailhead location: Map: p. 132

The north trailhead is at the Thumb Butte recreation site approximately 3 miles west of downtown Prescott. Travel west on Gurley Street for 2.5 miles to Thumb Butte Rd. Continue northwest on Thumb Butte Road for 1.5 miles to the recreation site. The trailhead is just across the road from the picnic area.

Road condition: Paved

Hiking time: 1 hour   *Length:* 1.75 miles for loop.

Difficulty: Moderate   *Use:* Heavy

Uses permitted: Hiking only.

Recommended season of use: All seasons

Maps, other resources: Prescott National Forest, west half; U.S.G.S. topographic 7.5' quad for Iron Springs.

Trail description:

We will describe this loop trail from the east and steeper leg to the west and more gentle leg of the loop. The east leg is quite steep with many switchbacks that traverse a fairly open terrain. The west leg is more gentle and stays for most of its length within a cool forested canyon.

Which leg you choose to ascend depends on several factors: your physical condition, weather, and your objective in hiking this trail. If, for example, you have trouble with knee joint pain on steep downhill hiking, you should probably ascend the steep leg. You might also want to ascend the steeper leg if the trail is covered with ice or snow, or if your objective in hiking this trail is physical conditioning.

At 0.2 miles you will come to the first of several good overlooks to the north. Granite Mountain occurs from this point on an azimuth of 358 degrees; Bill Williams Mountain, 22 degrees; the high point of Iron Springs Road just before it descends to Skull Valley, 295 degrees; and

Little Granite Mountain, 325 degrees. These azimuths assume that you have set a declination constant of 14 degrees on your compass. I learned recently that this magnetic declination has changed now to 12.5 degrees. The azimuths presented throughout this guide are based on the older reading of 14 degrees.

At 0.34 miles, after coming through a long series of switchbacks, you will pass a grove of deciduous Gambel oaks, a species that normally occurs above 6,500 feet.

At 0.6 miles you will reach the saddle below the basaltic dome of Thumb Butte. A narrow trail leaves the main trail here to the east and is an approach to the butte itself. Be aware, however, that the climb to the summit is quite dangerous, particularly if you are unacquainted with the routes to the summit. The east side of the butte is often used as a practice site by experienced climbers having the equipment and expertise to scale even sheer rock walls with comparative safety. Such places, however, are not meant for free-climbing (without ropes) and have proven fatal to reckless, inexperienced hikers.

The main trail goes west at this saddle but soon curves to the east, passing below the south side of Thumb Butte. It eventually heads west again. As you descend this south-facing warm slope you will be in a pinyon-juniper vegetation type, the pinyon being mainly the single-needle subspecies of this group.

At 0.8 miles you will come to a short narrow trail that goes to a good overlook of the Prescott area. At the end of this spur trail you will also note a grotesquely sculptured pinyon tree having a diameter of about 2.5 feet.

On the main trail, just beyond this spur trail there is a junction marked by an old yellow-painted sign that shows the direction to the Groom Creek Vista Point. It is just a short walk to this site and well worth the diversion. From this point your view of the horizon is blocked in only a small arc to the north. From left to right you can see the San Francisco Peaks, Mingus Mountain, Glassford Hill, city of Prescott, the ridges of the northern Bradshaw Mountains, and then the ridge of the Sierra Prietas. Wolverton Mountain lies along this ridge on an azimuth of 174 degrees, Mt. Francis at 190 degrees, Williams Peak at 230 degrees, and West Spruce Mountain at 268 degrees. Just to the

right of West Spruce Mountain is the residential development of Highland Pines.

As you return to the yellow sign, note also that it indicates that the return leg of the trail is in the direction from which we have just come. That interpretation of what constitutes the return leg depends, of course, on which leg of the trail you happened to ascend. Don't be confused by this suggestion that there is only one direction in which this trail can be traveled.

Scattered along the west leg of the trail are several interpretive signs identifying various native plants of this area.

At 0.8 miles the trail leaves the warm south-facing ridge and descends a north-facing slope within a cool forested drainage. Just beyond 1.0 miles you will see a sign on the west side of the trail identifying a large, yellow-bark ponderosa pine. This is a rare specimen in a forest of mostly second-growth pine.

At 1.5 miles you will pass through a squeaky turnstile. When I last hiked the trail there were lots of clippings of pine needle bundles, evidence of the work of the tassel-eared (Abert) squirrel. They chew the inner bark of terminal twigs, clipping off these needle bundles in the process.

The trail ends at 1.7 miles, back at the point from where you started on Thumb Butte Road.

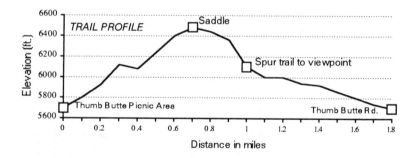

WILLOW CREEK TRAIL

General information:

This is a pleasant, short trail that connects the Thumb Butte Picnic Area and Pine Lakes and Kingswood residential areas. From the Thumb Butte area to the Forest boundary near Pine Lakes, the trail is used by horseback riders. However, riders cannot enter the trail from the Thumb Butte Picnic area, since horses are not permitted there. One can, however, reach this trail from other trails within the Prescott National Forest (e.g., Trail #317) or from private property along the old railroad grade bordering the north end of the trail.

Access and trailhead location: Map: p. 132

The south end of this trail can be approached by way of the Thumb Butte Picnic Area. Drive west from downtown Prescott on Gurley Street for 2.5 miles to Thumb Butte Rd. Continue northwest on Thumb Butte Rd. for 1.5 miles to the Thumb Butte recreation site and the picnic area. You then must travel for a short distance on Trail #316 and Trail #317 (see route description below). The trailhead for Trail #316 is just about 25 yards north of the three stone steps at picnic table #8. The trail description below uses this access.

To reach the trail from the Pine Lakes residential area, travel north from downtown Prescott on Montezuma Street for 1.75 miles to the 4-way intersection. Continue west on Iron Springs Road from this junction for another 2.6 miles to Hereford Drive, which is just opposite the turnoff to Wildwood Estates. Go south on Hereford Drive for a short distance to the Kingswood tennis courts. Turn west along West Pine Lakes Rd. to Pine Lakes residential area. Just after you pass the recreation hall continue straight on Alpine. When you come to Midway, turn right. Continue on Midway past two streets to Maverick. Turn right and continue for just a short distance to where the paved road exits the residential area onto a dirt road. This is a portion of the old railroad grade. Park on the dirt road and walk left (south). The trail leaves to the left of this road just a few feet past a cattle guard.

Road condition: Paved.

Hiking time: 1.5 hours

Length: 2.2 miles from Thumb Butte to Forest boundary on north; 3.1 miles to Pine Lakes residential area.

Difficulty: Easy.   *Use:* Moderate.

Uses permitted: Hiking and horseback riding only, although horses are not permitted within the Thumb Butte Picnic Area. The trail is also suitable for bicycling, at least as far as Willow Creek. The route within the creek, however, is probably too rough and rocky for cycling.

Recommended seasons of use: Spring, fall, winter. This route is likely to be quite warm on the hottest summer days.

Maps, other resources: Prescott National Forest, west half; U.S.G.S. topographic 7.5′ quad for Iron Springs.

Trail description:

To reach the Willow Creek Trail, you must travel Trail #316 and #317 for a short distance. Trail #316 starts at the northwest end of the Thumb Butte picnic area just north of Table #8. It travels almost due north from this point, passing through a gate at 0.1 miles. Since this portion of the trail ascends a south-facing slope, the area is quite open and sunny. Scrub oaks, manzanita, and pinyon pines dominate the landscape. Consequently, a hike started late on a summer day can be very warm.

At mile 0.3 there is a well-marked junction with Trail #317. Travel west on Trail #317. At mile 0.7 there is a conspicuous trail junction marked by a pile of rocks. Take the trail to the right (north). The trail from here into the Willow Creek drainage goes through heavy stands of mature brush (manzanita, New Mexico locust, small oaks) with an overstory of scattered ponderosa pines. The pines provide enough shade to make this a pleasant section of trail even on a warm day.

At mile 1.8 the trail drops into the Willow Creek drainage, a heavily scoured wash, yet with a good growth of small riparian trees and shrubs. Continue north along Willow Creek. For a short distance the trail stays along the east side of the creek, but then crosses the creek several times. From here to the Forest boundary the route follows the creek, but because the creek occasionally floods, the trail within the creek itself disappears. Where the trail appears to end at the creek, simply search the opposite bank to see where it exits the creek and continues on the other side.

At mile 2.2 the trail reaches the Forest boundary, marked with a small yellow sign. From here to Pine Lakes parts of the route are on private property, although I encountered no signs prohibiting travel.

Continuing north you will soon come to a spot where the creek narrows as it passes between rock walls. Water passing over this hard rock shelf has beautifully sculptured the dark gray rock into sinuous flow channels and small plunge pools.

Here you have a choice of routes. A route to the left skirts the Emmanuel Pines Camp and the west side of the Pine Lakes residential area. To travel this route, follow the small drainage west away from Willow Creek. You will quickly come to a dirt road. Follow the trail that parallels the road but to the right. Within 0.1 miles this trail leaves the road, climbing to the right up a small hill.

At 2.4 miles you will reach a trail junction marked with rock "V." Stay to the left; the right fork goes to an overlook above the rocky narrows. At 2.6 miles you will pass a wire gate next to the trail. This is an access point from the Pine Lakes area (Jct. Westgate and Midway Rds.). This fence also marks the boundary between the Prescott National Forest and the residential area. Continue northwest staying to the left of the wire fence but within sight of Pine Lake residences. At 3.1 miles you will reach the dirt road which goes to the Emmanuel Pine Camp. Stay right on this road past a cattle guard and past a locked cable across the road. Just beyond the cable is the parking area described above for a north access to the trail.

At the rocky narrows, an alternate route goes north, staying in the Willow Creek drainage and skirting the east side of Pine Lakes. At 2.8 miles you will come to a wide clearing, the ground in fall covered with a blanket of small yellow flowers. This site apparently was a homestead or other human habitation as evidenced by rock walls and steps, building foundations, and walkways. About 100 yards east of this site in a small tributary wash is a rock wall perhaps 15 feet in height. This site likely creates a spectacular waterfall during periods of heavy rainfall and runoff.

At 2.9 miles as you approach residences within the Pine Lakes area, you will encounter remnants of a barbed-wire fence across the wash. Just beyond this fence on the west bank is a good place to exit the wash. There is a short cobbled walkway that passes between two residences to the paved road.

You can also reach the Pine Lakes Road by continuing north along Willow Creek. The creek from here narrows considerably, passing through thick stands of willow before reaching the bridged roadway. There is no trail along this 0.2-mile stretch of creek and travel is in the creekbed.

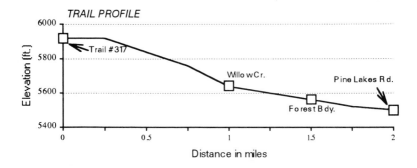

LONG'S CANYON TRAIL #316
RIDGE TRAIL #317
THUMB BUTTE TRAIL #33
WILLOW CREEK TRAIL

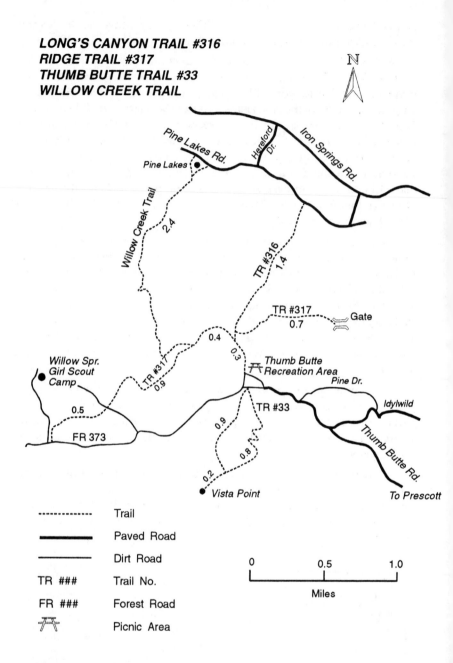

N

Pine Lakes Rd.

Hereford Dr.

Iron Springs Rd.

Pine Lakes

Willow Creek Trail

2.4

TR #316
1.4

TR #317
0.7 ⊨ Gate

0.4

0.3

Thumb Butte
Recreation Area

Pine Dr.

Idylwild

Willow Spr.
Girl Scout
Camp

TR #317
0.9

TR #33

0.5

0.9

Thumb Butte Rd.

FR 373

0.8

To Prescott

0.2

Vista Point

---------- Trail

▬▬▬▬ Paved Road

──── Dirt Road

TR ### Trail No.

FR ### Forest Road

🅿 Picnic Area

0	0.5	1.0

Miles

Selected References

Outdoor Recreation

Aitchison, Stewart. *A Guide to Exploring Oak Creek and the Sedona Area*. RNM Press, Salt Lake City, UT. 1989.

Aitchison, Stewart and Bruce Grubbs. *The Hiker's Guide to Arizona*. Falcon Press, Helena & Billings, MT. 1991.

Baille, Rowan. *Prescott Trails*. Prescott, AZ. 1992.

Mangum, Richard K. and Sherry G. Mangum. *Flagstaff Hikes and Mountain Bike Rides*. Hexagon Press, Flagstaff, AZ. 1992.

Maurer, Stephen G. (editor). *Visitors Guide: Kaibab National Forest: Williams, Chalender & Tusayan Ranger Districts*. SNCHA, Albuquerque, NM. 1990.

Mazel, David. *Arizona Trails: 100 Hikes in Canyon and Sierra*. Wilderness Press, Berkeley, CA. 1991.

Slingluff, Jim. *Verde River Recreation Guide*. Golden West Publishers, Phoenix, AZ. 1990.

Wildlife

Carr, John N. Arizona *Wildlife Viewing Guide*. Falcon Press, Helena & Billings, MT. 1992.

Halfpenny, James. *A Field Guide to Mammal Tracking in North America*. Johnson Books, Boulder, CO. 1986.

Scott, Shirley L. (editor) *Field Guide to the Birds of North America*. National Geographic Society, Wash. D.C. 1983.

Plants

Dodge, Natt N. *Flowers of the Southwest Deserts*. Southwest Parks and Monuments Assoc., Tucson, AZ. 1992.

Elmore, Francis H. *Shrubs and Trees of the Southwest Uplands*. Southwest Parks and Monuments Assoc., Tucson, AZ. 1987.

Foxx, Teralene S. and Dorothy Hoard. *Flowers of the Southwest Forests and Woodlands*. Los Alamos Historical Society, Los Alamos, NM. 1984.

Geology

Chronic, Halka. *Roadside Geology of Arizona*. Mountain Press Publ. Co., Missoula, MT. 1992.

Nations, D. and E. Stump. *Geology of Arizona*. Kendall & Hunt Publ. Co., Dubuque, IA. 1981.

Colophon

The manuscript for this field guide was prepared in WordPerfect 5.1. The page formatting was done in Windows Version of Ventura Publisher 3.0. Body text was set in ITC Garamond with headings in Futura Bold. Cover was designed in CorelDraw 4.0. Camera-ready copy was printed on an HP LaserJet IIIP.

Page Layout: Ronald H. Smith, Castle Rock Publishing

Pen & Ink Illustrations: Dee Cantlon, Graphic Designer & Illustrator

Copyediting: Jerry Ellsworth

Printing: Graphic Impressions, Inc., 444 W. Sheldon, Suite A, Prescott, AZ 86301.

Notes

Notes